God's Got You Covered:
20 Keys for Your Protection

God's Got You Covered:
20 Keys for Your Protection

By
Rod Parsley

RESULTS
PUBLISHING

Columbus, Ohio

TABLE OF CONTENTS:

This know also, that in the last days perilous times shall come. For men shall be lovers of their own selves, covetous, boasters, proud, blasphemers, disobedient to parents, unthankful, unholy, Without natural affection, trucebreakers, false accusers, incontinent, fierce, despisers of those that are good, Traitors, heady, highminded, lovers of pleasures more than lovers of God; Having a form of godliness, but denying the power thereof: from such turn away. For of this sort are they which creep into houses, and lead captive silly women laden with sins, led away with divers lusts, Ever learning, and never able to come to the knowledge of the truth.

—2 Timothy 3:1-7

INTRODUCTION:
A PROPHETIC CALL TO REALITY

I have a prophetic word for you: troubled times are upon us! Many people read the above passage and say, "Well, Pastor Rod, times have always been perilous. What makes this time in history any different?"

What makes this time different is that never before in the history of mankind has such potential existed for our own destruction. We saw it on the fateful day of Sept. 11, 2001, when religious extremists used jet airplanes as bombs, killing thousands of people. In the city where I live, we have seen it in a string of shootings along our highways, where an anonymous shooter has been using passing vehicles for target practice. We see it in the ongoing threat of global war. I've been told that hydrogen bombs are so powerful, they require an atomic bomb to detonate them! Scientists claim that if a large hydrogen bomb ever exploded in our earth's atmosphere, the shock could cause an imbalance which would bring civilization, as we know it, to a standstill.

Times have always been perilous, but this is perhaps the most perilous time of all!

Men and women "without natural affection" are engaging in homosexual and lesbian activity despite the end-time generation's plague of AIDS—a killer that man has slowed down, but has not been able to stop. AIDS-infected people

7

who are "lovers of pleasure" continue to have sex at any cost with multiple partners, without ever informing them about their HIV infections. These "lovers of their own selves" want self-gratification in sex—even if it means DEATH to their partners! They also want to equate their relationships with the God-ordained ordinance of marriage, and misguided judges and politicians are clamoring to give it to them.

We have never seen a time like this!

Significant elements within the secular media have become open "despisers of those that are good," constantly showing Christianity in a negative light and refusing to depict any Christian as intelligent, warm, considerate, or loving.

America was founded on a strong belief in the guiding hand of God. Yet today, that belief is being pushed aside by belief instead in self-interest and self-indulgence. The message of the last decade in America has been to "do our own thing" and "just be happy," yet we suddenly wake up to a nation where prayer is yanked out of schools, nativity scenes are forbidden in many public parks, and traditional Christmas songs cannot be sung at many public school Christmas celebrations. Well-meaning people even shy away from wishing each other "Merry Christmas" in the last weeks of the year for fear of offending someone. When did Christmas, of all things, become a taboo subject?

America has become a moral wasteland, where half of all marriages end in divorce—where men and women who have become "lovers of pleasures more than lovers of God" are willing to sacrifice their marriage covenants on the altar of self-indulgent pleasure.

Our country is exploding with "growth groups" that put you "in touch" with the god-you—not the Creator God we know, but the you who is supposedly a god. They talk about inner strength, inner self-fulfillment and hundreds of other lofty-sounding terms. But the stark reality is these groups operate without knowledge of the one true God, and they portray a mere "form of godliness."

We have never seen a day like today! Television programs portray all types of sexual behavior, with little thought to the holy bonds of marriage. These programs are not harmless; the endless display of sculpted bodies in soap operas, music videos, and evening dramas, seeking instant sexual gratification, cannot compare with our real lives. But they are presented as normal and natural, and they raise in us desires many people are not prepared to resist. No wonder adultery is an increasing problem in our society today.

Clearly, TV is "creeping into homes" and presenting situations to take men and women captive "with divers lusts." The writers of these programs often portray sinful liaisons as morally neutral, with few, if any, negative results.

Our children, just reaching the age of puberty, are "educated" on how to use condoms so they can practice "safe sex." But they are never counseled about the emotional or moral traumas that can result from sexual relationships at an early age. These same children are then "counseled" on how to secure an abortion without parental permission, yet they cannot go to the school nurse and get an aspirin without a note from their parents!

We are living in a uniquely evil day! America has stopped making any moral sense.

We have the most modern technological advances to save lives in the history of the universe. Yet an unborn child is aborted every twenty-one seconds.

We have the most advanced printing presses and computer typesetting ever available to publish the Word of God and materials that exalt His name. We have sophisticated computer networks that make it possible to access the wisdom of godly men from centuries past right up to the present day. Yet instead, those resources are used to publish and distribute pornography. These materials exploit the women and children who appear in them; the (predominantly) men who take in these vile images and use them to feed their unnatural fantasies; and the families whose lives are destroyed from others' addiction to it. Even pastors have become victims of Internet pornography! Times have always been perilous, but this is by far the most perilous of all times!

This book is intended to awaken and encourage you to a prophetic reality. Like the prophet Isaiah,

> The Lord God hath given me the tongue of the learned, that I should know how to speak a word in season to him that is weary: he wakeneth morning by morning, he wakeneth mine ear to hear as the learned.
>
> —Isaiah 50:4

Friend, there is hope for you beyond the scope of human limitation!

To find this prophetic reality, we must look to the Word of God. If you look to America for hope, you will find a moral wasteland of empty promises and vanishing dreams. America can no longer cope with exploding catastrophes in the cities and in the nation. The boiling, brewing caldron of racial hatred explodes time and time again in our cities.

Our nation's governmental policies often reflect our twisted priorities. We live in a nation where a few owls become more important than the welfare of tens of thousands of families, and where a few whales are more valuable than the lives of millions of aborted babies. Instead of prioritizing the spiritual welfare of our citizens, and the care of the neediest among us, we focus instead on the material needs of those who already are comfortable.

Yes, America is a mess. This is truly the most perilous time of all!

It is time for us to refuse to allow our future to be dominated or dictated to by the flesh, according to human limitations. It is time for us to lift our eyes beyond the seen into the unseen; we must see what cannot be seen, and hear what cannot be heard.

The apostle Paul wrote,

> While we look not at the things which are seen, but at the things which are not seen: for the things which are seen are temporal; but the things which are not seen are eternal.
>
> —2 Corinthians 4:18

This is a paradox. How do we look at something that cannot be seen? We must know the answer to survive in America's end-time cuture. We must look to the God who created us and bought our redemption through the suffering and death of His Son, Jesus Christ. We must look to the God who has us covered!

We must look to God to face temptation, to conquer cancer, to cast off the attacks of anti-Christians and to survive the financial failures all around us.

We must know how to survive the perils of perilous times, just as the apostle Paul did. From a prison cell, Paul wrote,

> I know both how to be abased, and I know how to abound: every where and in all things I am instructed both to be full and to be hungry, both to abound and to suffer need. I can do all things through Christ which strengtheneth me.
>
> —Philippians 4:12,13

In this passage, Paul declared,

> I have been in the perils of the deep, in the perils of my countrymen, and in the perils of affliction; I have been in the middle of the desert; I have been left for dead! But I have learned how to survive.

This Is not a Popular Message!

I know you would rather read a message that tells you things are going to get better. I would prefer to deliver that message. But the Bible gives us the opposite message. The Bible tells us things are not going to get better. Instead, things are going to get worse! But God has you covered; He is here to protect you and nurture you and love you in the midst of your perilous times. There is hope for your discouragement!

Even Elijah became discouraged. The Bible says,

> But he himself went a day's journey into the wilderness, and came and sat down under a juniper tree: and he requested for himself that he might die; and said, It is enough; now, O Lord, take away my life; for I am not better than my fathers.
>
> —1 Kings 19:4

And this period of depression came just after Elijah had come through the greatest victory of his ministry.

Always remember this: your greatest conflict will come on the heels of your greatest victory. The peril of the mountain top is that when you are there, you have the delusion that you are always going to be there.

Elijah was a man of God, and God sent His angel to minister to him:

> And as he lay and slept under a juniper tree, behold, then an angel touched him, and said unto him, Arise and eat. And he looked, and, behold, there was a cake baken on the coals, and a cruse of water at his head. And he did eat and drink, and laid him down again.
>
> —1 Kings 19:5,6

The kingdom of God is not all mountain tops! There are going to be some valleys. The same God who ministered to Elijah is standing ready to meet your every need. He has you covered!

Every now and then there is a cup of sorrow to drink. When sorrow does come into your life—and it will—do not take the popular and immature stance running around in many Christian circles that says, "Anything that is discomforting to my flesh comes from the devil." That is nonsense. Go beyond that limited teaching, and realize that though your latest challenge may have come from the devil, you are walking a consecrated life. You are walking the highway of holiness. Your steps are ordered of the Lord. Whatever you step into may not have come from the Lord, but it was allowed by your Father. He is molding you as a potter molds the clay. If you will allow it, your present difficulty will produce Christlikeness in you.

Paul was a man who knew how to survive the perils of perilous times. He knew that there was hope beyond the hope of human limitation—both for him and for everyone who crossed the path of his life.

We need to get beyond the mentality that all we have to do is to "get up in the morning and rebuke the devil." We need to do something before we rebuke the devil.

13

James 4:7 does not only say, "Resist the devil, and he will flee from you." It says, "Submit yourselves therefore to God. Resist the devil, and he will flee from you." Submitting to God comes first. Submitting says, "I yield my control to God. I will no longer take the Word of God and try to get my own way with it."

In Genesis 32:24-31, Jacob saw God face-to-face. He was then a marked man—he walked differently, everyone could see that he had been with God.

I want to be like Jacob. I want people to see that I have been in the presence of God, in contact with the great I AM!

We need to understand that because we live in perilous times, we will face perils. "Well, Pastor Rod," you say, "I can't believe God would let this difficulty come into my life." But it is inevitable that we will have tribulation; Jesus promised His disciples they would bear trials, and we should expect no less. We should be proud to suffer for Him, because He can use our sufferings to draw others to Himself. Jesus is looking for people who will stand up for Him, even when a cup of sorrow comes their way.

The apostle Paul encouraged us to maintain our faith in the face of difficulty. He wrote,

> Brethren, I count not myself to have apprehended: but this one thing I do, forgetting those things which are behind, and reaching forth unto those things which are before, I press toward the mark for the prize of the high calling of God in Christ Jesus.
> —Philippians 3:13,14

Paul was telling the Philippians, "I'm focusing on Christ. If you want to follow anything, follow the way I'm following Him. Do not follow me, but follow my following. Follow the way that I trust in Him when I'm walking through the fire. Follow the way I reach out for a hand bigger than my hand. Follow my following."

As you read this, you may be facing the greatest trials and conflicts of your life. And the way you respond to those trials and conflicts will have a profound influence on your friends, family and co-workers—possibly in ways that are not immediately apparent to you. As a Spirit-filled Christian you set an example for others with the way you respond to trials. You can believe that others will "follow your following." That alone is reason to believe that God has you covered, even in the midst of your trials.

Be a Modern-Day 'Survivor'

> Whose voice then shook the earth: but now he hath promised, saying, Yet once more I shake not the earth only, but also heaven. And this word, Yet once more, signifieth the removing of those things that are shaken, as of things that are made, that those things which cannot be shaken may remain.
> —Hebrews 12:26,27

There are people right now who are losing their careers for no other reason than they are Christians. We must learn how to survive!

A group of judges in Massachusetts has decided that they know better than centuries of legislators and politicians, and that the time-tested model of marriage between a man and a woman is inadequate. Homosexuals are very close to having the right to marry. In San Francisco, the mayor even granted that right in early 2004, in defiance of a state law enacted by a significant majority of California citizens. In many states, laws even require churches to hire homosexuals, if they are qualified for the jobs that are available. Our desire to enforce what we believe to be a moral standard is not a consideration. We must learn how to survive!

In Russia, the Holy Bible can be taught in the classrooms. But in America, a public school teacher cannot even put a copy of the Ten Commandments up in the classroom. We must learn how to survive!

Women's rights groups can freely advocate a radical, godless agenda in public forums without criticism. But when Christians mobilize, we are accused by the media of trying to "force" our will on others. It seems the only socially acceptable form of bigotry is bigotry against evangelical Christians. We must learn how to survive!

The Holy Spirit once inspired someone to write,

> But ye are come unto mount Sion, and unto the city of the living God, the heavenly Jerusalem, and to an innumerable company of angels.
> —Hebrews 12:22

That verse tells us we have come into the realm of the Spirit, which lies beyond the horizon of human perception. The only way for you to access that realm is in the Spirit.

That is how Paul, who learned to survive the perils of perilous times, found himself imprisoned in the sewage systems of Rome, and yet he said,

> Blessed be the God and Father of our Lord Jesus Christ, who hath blessed us with all spiritual blessings in heavenly places in Christ.
> —Ephesians 1:3

When Paul wrote these words, he was not sitting in a mansion with a multitude of servants waiting upon his every desire. He was in prison!

But Paul said, "God hath raised me up."

To survive the perils of perilous times, you have to learn that your natural circumstances do not dictate your spiritual altitude. In the natural, your body can be in the flatlands with the ducks while your spirit is soaring across the snowcapped peaks of mighty mountains with the eagle nature of the Spirit of God!

> To the general assembly and church of the first-born, which are written in heaven, and to God the Judge of all, and to the spirits of just men made perfect, And to Jesus the mediator of the new covenant, and to the blood of sprinkling, that speaketh better things than that of Abel. See that ye refuse not him that speaketh. For if they escaped not who refused him that spake on earth, much more shall not we escape, if we turn away from him that speaketh from heaven: Whose voice then shook the earth: but now he hath promised, saying, Yet once more I shake not the earth only, but also heaven. And this word, Yet once more, signifieth the removing of those things that are shaken, as of things that are made, that those things which cannot be shaken may remain.
>
> —Hebrews 12:23-27

Paul was declaring, "We are part of this thing we call the natural realm; and the only thing that is going to survive this shaking is not what is born of the flesh, and not what is founded on flesh, but rather that which is born of the Spirit."

You are born of the Spirit of God; you are not just a natural man.

When His Son lay wrapped in grave clothes in the borrowed tomb of Joseph of Arimathaea, and while the demon hordes of hell howled and cackled in the bowels of perdition,

God did not hang His head. When hell had done its worst to the best that heaven had to offer, God raised Him from the dead, proving and loudly proclaiming that there is hope beyond the confines of mortality! And, we have a rightful claim to that hope, because we are children of God.

Stand on the sandy shore and look out as far as your eye can see, and see that place where heaven kisses earth and the sea caresses the glory of the heavens.

Look as far as you can see from that same sandy beach, and suddenly, you will see something pop up over the edge of what you can see with your natural eye.

Jesus was the seed of David according to the flesh, but just over the horizon, just beyond what could be seen with human eyes, was the miraculous resurrection from the dead!

He surfaced beyond the border of mortal man's domain when He kicked the end out of the tomb and resurrected with power, triumphing over death, hell and the grave.

There is hope for you beyond the scope of human limitation, but you are not going to experience it just looking in the natural all the time and letting your feelings dictate how you will respond to your circumstances. "Well," you say, "it's just so gloomy today." So what? There is a limitless hope living on the inside of you!

You may be required to walk through the lonesome valley. Jesus went through the trial of perilous times; He went into the grave, but He came out victorious on the other side.

Seek That Which Endures

The things you see are temporal, subject to change. There are only three things that endure.

• First, the graces of God. "And now abideth faith, hope, charity, these three; but the greatest of these is charity"

(1 Corinthians 13:13). Faith, hope, and charity will endure and will sustain you through the perils of perilous times.

• Second, the unseen things of the spirit realm. That is the reason the Word endures. "Heaven and earth shall pass away, but my words shall not pass away" (Matthew 24:35).

• Third, the kingdom of God. "Wherefore we receiving a kingdom which cannot be moved, let us have grace, whereby we may serve God acceptably with reverence and godly fear" (Hebrews 12:28).

You are part of a kingdom which cannot be shaken, cannot be removed and cannot fall apart. It is going to endure! You are going to be there when the new Jerusalem, 1,500 miles square, comes down out of the very being of God; you get to live there!

> Forasmuch then as the children are partakers of
> flesh and blood, he also himself likewise took part of
> the same; that through death he might destroy him
> that had the power of death, that is, the devil.
> —Hebrews 2:14

God's got you covered. His blood covers you. You are blood-bought into a supernatural kingdom that cannot be moved. The only time you have to fear anything is when you step outside that kingdom.

The devil is a thief; he does not have to be strong. All he has to do is catch you "not at home" in the realm of the spirit.

Read This Book Prayerfully

As you prayerfully read these essential keys to God's protection, remember,

> God is our refuge and strength, a very present help in trouble. Therefore will not we fear, though the earth be removed, and though the mountains be carried into the midst of the sea; Though the waters thereof roar and be troubled, though the mountains shake with the swelling thereof.
>
> —Psalm 46:1-3

Right now, you may feel like your world is falling apart. Remember Psalm 46. God will preserve you in the midst of trouble.

Many Christians want to stick their heads in the sand and pretend everything in life is just beautiful.

But how can life be beautiful when 4,500 babies a day are being stripped out of the wombs of their mothers? How can life be beautiful when people will protest another country's policies by hijacking planes and flying them into buildings full of people? How can life be beautiful when lesbianism and homosexuality are portrayed as "normal" lifestyles? Something is wrong.

Preachers are scorned; churches are dead and cold. There is a seeming dearth of the prophetic Word of God in the earth. Things do not look good.

But God says, in the midst of perilous times, "Sit down a minute; relax. See the whole picture."

Psalm 46 continues:

> There is a river, the streams whereof shall make glad the city of God, the holy place of the tabernacles of the most High. God is in the midst of her; she shall not be moved: God shall help her, and that right early.
>
> —Psalm 46:4,5

There is a river of God which shall make you glad, even in the midst of perilous circumstances. This book will show you how to swim in that river!

In the last days, God promises to pour out His Spirit on all flesh. Doctor Luke quoted the prophet Joel as follows:

> And it shall come to pass in the last days, saith God, I will pour out of my Spirit upon all flesh: and your sons and your daughters shall prophesy, and your young men shall see visions, and your old men shall dream dreams: And on my servants and on my handmaidens I will pour out in those days of my Spirit; and they shall prophesy: And I will shew wonders in heaven above, and signs in the earth beneath; blood, and fire, and vapour of smoke.
>
> —Acts 2:17-19

God is going to turn up the heat, but you will be swimming in the living water of the Holy Spirit!

> Be glad then, ye children of Zion, and rejoice in the Lord your God: for he hath given you the former rain moderately, and he will cause to come down for you the rain, the former rain, and the latter rain in the first month. And the floors shall be full of wheat, and the fats shall overflow with wine and oil.
>
> —Joel 2:23,24

There is a Holy Spirit flood coming; get ready to jump in! While the banks of the world are failing, get ready, because your house will overflow with oil and be full with wheat! Jump in the river of the precious Holy Ghost.

Feed Your Spirit Man

So many Christians appear strong and healthy on the outside, but on the inside they are emaciated creatures—their elbows bigger than their arms, their knees sticking out bigger than their thighs, theirs eyes sunk back in their skulls, barely able to move.

Their spirits are weak and tired. Why? Because they are not feeding the spirit man.

Many claim that they want to be "spiritual giants," but they spend all their time feeding the natural man—the man who died when they accepted Christ.

In these perilous times, your natural man cannot cope with the circumstances. You will feel like pulling your hair out by the roots, and your little trembling hand will reach out for a hand bigger than yours—but there will be no hand to grab, no place to turn.

At that needy moment, you will turn to your spirit and ask your spirit to respond as though you have been feeding him three times a day, when you barely feed him three times a week!

The Bible says,

> For which cause we faint not; but though our outward man perish, yet the inward man is renewed day by day.
> —2 Corinthians 4:16

Do you want to know how to successfully navigate the perils of perilous times? Read, believe, and put into action the keys for protection contained in this book.

When you understand how God longs to protect you, the Holy Ghost will safely navigate you down a river of peace while others all around you are drowning. When your husband walks in and says, "I do not happen to like your looks anymore. I'm leaving you," God has a river of living water for you. When the doctor looks at you and says, "You have to die; you cannot live with this cancer," there are streams of living water that run straight from the city of God and the tabernacles of the Most High to you.

When you are going through the perils of perilous times, your spirit man can grasp hold of the anchor of the Word of the Almighty and say, "This is it. I do not care what it looks like, sounds like, smells like, or feels like. I can see beyond this circumstance, and there is hope beyond that scope."

If you are going to survive, you need to stir up your spirit and grasp hold of this Word. I do not care what you are facing as you read this book, or what you will face tomorrow. If you will apply the spiritual principles contained in these keys for God's protection, you will be victorious.

Here are three facts to keep in mind as you read:

1. Perilous times are coming.

2. You are a spirit being.

3. God's Word is infallible.

If you are going to survive these perilous times, you are going to have to realize you are a spirit man. Become intimately acquainted with the Spirit of the Living God, and be led by His Spirit. The spiritually dead are led by their head. Start to be led by your spirit.

The Word is the oak of God planted in the forest of eternity, entwining its roots around the Rock of Ages. Take hold of God's Word. Though heaven and earth pass away, though the world be on fire, you will stand and watch it burn. You will successfully navigate the trials of perilous times.

As you recognize these three facts and begin to apply these keys for protection to your own life, your victory will be assured!

Therefore if any man be in Christ, he is a new creature: old things are passed away; behold, all things are become new.

—2 Corinthians 5:17

If you are going to survive the onslaught of hell in the last days, make sure you are born again to the bone.

—Pastor Rod Parsley

KEY 1:
BE BORN AGAIN—TO THE BONE

John Townsend wrote a letter to Queen Victoria, urging her to read John 3:16 and Romans 10:9-10, so she might know that the eternal life promised in the Bible is sure both for the present and the future.

About two weeks later, Townsend received the following reply, signed by the queen: "Your letter of recent date received, and in reply I would state that I have carefully and prayerfully read the portions of Scripture referred to. I believe in the finished work of Christ for me, and trust by God's grace to meet you in that Home of which He said, 'I go to prepare a place for you.'"

The first key to God's protection is salvation! You need to be born again! If you are going to survive the onslaught of hell in these last days, make sure you are born again to the bone. There is salvation in no other name except the name of Jesus Christ of Nazareth.

There is no salvation in a Shinto shrine or a Buddhist temple. You can lick a crystal until your tongue falls out, and it will not get you into the gates of the Heavenly City. There is no salvation in a New Age god. There is only one way to obtain salvation, and that is through trusting in the blood-stained cross of Jesus Christ!

The apostle Paul wrote,

> Wherefore God also hath highly exalted him,
> and given him a name which is above every name:
> That at the name of Jesus every knee should bow, of
> things in heaven, and things in earth, and things
> under the earth; And that every tongue should con-
> fess that Jesus Christ is Lord, to the glory of God the
> Father.
>
> —Philippians 2:9-11

Many in the church have an incomplete and inadequate
view of what salvation is and what it does. Salvation is not
just walking down an aisle or signing a piece of paper or
going to a neighborhood church. It is not resolving to be a
nice person. You will never get to heaven by paying your
taxes, or by being an upstanding person in the community.
There is only one way to heaven! Jesus said,

> I am the way, the truth, and the life: no man
> cometh unto the Father, but by me.
>
> —John 14:6

Nicodemus, a member of the ruling class of his day,
came to Jesus seeking God. Jesus told him,

> Verily, verily, I say unto thee, Except a man be
> born again, he cannot see the kingdom of God.
>
> —John 3:3

Alive in Christ

C.M. Ward said:
"Anything alive must have an appetite.

Anything alive must have discharge.
Anything alive must have growth.
Anything alive must have reproduction."

If you are alive through Christ Jesus, if you are a new creature through the born-again salvation experience, then these four areas will manifest themselves in your life.

• You will have an appetite to know all you can about the nature of God, through His Word. "Blessed are they which do hunger and thirst after righteousness; for they shall be filled" (Matthew 5:16).

• You will desire to discharge, to put away all the things that excite the world but are not profitable to God. "He that loveth his life shall lose it; and he that hateth his life in this world shall keep it unto life eternal" (John 12:25).

• You will have the desire to grow each day in those things which bring you closer to the nature of Jesus Christ. "As newborn babes, desire the sincere milk of the word, that ye may grow thereby" (1 Peter 2:2).

• You will manifest reproduction through your evangelistic calling to bring your neighbors and friends to the Lord, to become sons of God. "And he said unto them, Go ye into all the world, and preach the gospel to every creature" (Mark 16:15).

When you accept the miraculous gift of salvation through faith in our Lord Jesus Christ, your appetites and your allegiances change.

Satan Hates His Own Children

Do not play around with your salvation.

You are either a child of the devil or a child of God; and you should know the devil hates his own kids. Satan will use you, abuse you, and destroy you as long as you play around in his kingdom. Jesus said of our adversary,

> The thief cometh not, but for to steal, and to kill, and to destroy: [but] I am come that they might have life, and that they might have it more abundantly.
> —John 10:10

The devil promises a rainbow, but delivers rain. He promises the world, but delivers hell. He is a liar. In fact, he is the very father of lies. Jesus once rebuked the Pharisees by saying,

> Ye are of your father the devil, and the lusts of your father ye will do. He was a murderer from the beginning, and abode not in the truth, because there is no truth in him. When he speaketh a lie, he speaketh of his own: for he is a liar, and the father of it.
> —John 8:44

Salvation Means "Whole In God"

Jesus' crucifixion and resurrection purchased salvation for us. One of the Greek words that is translated as "salvation" has a much broader meaning than many people think. That word is "sozo," pronounced "sode-zo." It means "to deliver, protect, heal, make whole, preserve, and do well by."

We need to get as close to God as we can in this end-time hour of spiritual history. We must allow the full manifestation of salvation in every area of our lives.

As Satan's attack intensifies, the children of God need to know how to pray, and then do it.

> He shall call upon me, and I will answer him: I

will be with him in trouble; I will deliver him, and honour him.

—Psalm 91:15

The children of God need to know how to give, and then do it.

Give, and it shall be given unto you; good measure, pressed down, and shaken together, and running over, shall men give into your bosom. For with the same measure that ye mete withal it shall be measured to you again.

—Luke 6:38

The children of God need to know how to fast, and then do it. Just as Hannah fasted and prayed year after year until she received a word from God and the answer to her prayer; so also do the saints of God need to learn how fasting and praying can bring God's word and answers into the struggles and trials of their lives. (See 1 Samuel 1.)

The children of God need to know how to live right, and then do it.

Neither yield ye your members as instruments of unrighteousness unto sin: but yield yourselves unto God, as those that are alive from the dead, and your members as instruments of righteousness unto God.

—Romans 6:13

To spiritually survive, it is vital for you to have an up-to-date relationship with the King of kings and the Lord of lords, because the devil hates everything about you. He despises you, and he will bring all hell to bear on your life to destroy you. The apostle Peter admonished us,

Be sober, be vigilant; because your adversary the devil, as a roaring lion, walketh about, seeking whom he may devour.

—1 Peter 5:8

Your only hope is to run out of the darkness and run into the light—to be born again by the Spirit of God—and get translated out of the kingdom of darkness and into the kingdom of Light. Only then will you come under God's protection. Only then will you be able to know—really know — that God's got you covered.

Desperate Times Demand Desperate Action

We are living in the last days. If you think the devil is not angry, you are wrong. He has honed his sights in on the church. The church is detestable in his sight; he hates it. Satan hates every person who names the name of Christ, and he especially hates the blood-bought, Holy Ghost-filled crowd that is not backing up to him.

This is not the time to fold your hands, to let your head hang down, to be sad or to roll your eyes like a dying calf and be religious. This is the time that the earth should break forth into praise and the mountains and the hills should break forth into singing!

Everyone who is covered with the precious blood of Christ must release the power that lives within them!

You may say, "That is too emotional, Pastor Rod. I can just stand here quietly and praise the Lord." Well, yes, you can. And in doing so, you can watch the devil steal your kids, send your business rocking and reeling into bankruptcy, or manifest some fatal cancer or other disease upon you. But it doesn't have to be that way. You can decide to counter the devil's schemes against you by relying on the Creator who saved you from a lifetime of separation from Him. It's your choice.

Desperate times demand desperate action.

The devil has already devised a plan for your tomorrow, so thwart his plan today. With everything that is in you, praise Him for your salvation that allows you to walk victoriously through these perilous times.

> Whoever speaks, as one who speaks oracles of God; whoever serves, as one who serves by the strength that God supplies — in order that in everything God may be glorified through Jesus Christ. To him belong glory and dominion forever and ever. Amen.
>
> —1 Peter 4:11

> If we can receive a revelation of who Jesus is, we can take our place in the kingdom, and the gates of hell will not prevail against us!"
>
> —Pastor Rod Parsley

You and I are fighting a spiritual war. We need to realize we are in a war and fight accordingly. The devil loves to do battle against men and women who aren't aware of the battle raging around them. Don't be deceived!

The first century church had to pray Simon Peter out of trouble time and time again because Satan had targeted him as a key man to attack.

When Herod sent forth his soldiers to persecute certain men in the church, one of those he particularly wanted to persecute was Peter—because Peter knew who Jesus was, and he was considered a spiritual field general.

Jesus asked Peter, "But whom say ye that I am?" (Matthew 16:15)

Without a moment's hesitation, the great fisherman replied, "Thou art the Christ, the Son of the living God" (Matthew 16:16).

> And Jesus answered and said unto him, Blessed art thou, Simon Barjona: for flesh and blood hath not revealed it unto thee, but my Father which is in heaven. And I say also unto thee, That thou art Peter, and upon this rock I will build my church; and the gates of hell shall not prevail against it.
>
> —Matthew 16:17,18

Because Peter knew who God was, and because God had a purpose for Peter, the enemy especially targeted him as a source of attack.

Do you ever wonder why the same devil that attacked Peter is always picking on you? Because you know too much!

He is not worried about the people that sing the first, second, and last verses of some dried-up old song in an ancient hymnal—or the latest upbeat praise chorus—as though they were just words on a page.

He is not worried about the people who are content to listen to some six-foot icicle stand up in the pulpit to moan and groan and hurriedly deliver a twenty-minute sermon. Those people don't give him anything to worry about!

Satan is worried about people who know the nature of Jesus, and are willing to serve Him as generals in God's end-time army. He is only worried about those who are serious about making it all the way to the heavenly city. He is only worried about those who are serious about depopulating the corridors of hell and increasing the population of heaven.

I want to encourage you to take your place in God's army and in the kingdom of God, where the gates of hell will not prevail against you in any manner, shape, or form.

Spiritual warfare is not a game, and the devil is not some innocent puppy. He is the master deceiver, thief, and murderer. He is the force behind all evil. He is the gnawing of cancer, the dollar bill in the pocket of the abortion doctor, the blank stare in the face of the homeless. He is the cold ache of arthritis, the limp of a crippled limb, the despair of poverty. He is the panic of sirens, the overcrowding of county jails, state prisons, and federal penitentiaries; he is the source of arguing, insanity, slander, lying, cheating, stealing, heresy, and sedition.

He is the reality and the necessity of an eternal hell.

He is behind every case of rape and incest. He is the perpetrator of all types of prejudice and slavery. He is the multiplied hideousness of Adolf Hitler and Osama bin Laden. He is suicide, teen pregnancy, the occult, demonic possession, and New Age deceit.

He is the original instigator of separation between the Creator and His creation. Yet we try to act and live like he is not even in our world! To survive the devil's attacks, you must realize that spiritual warfare is not a game, and that the devil is a real enemy, hell-bent on destroying you.

You need to understand that the devil is out to stop you, and that by relying on the God who has you covered, you can rebuke him and keep him from hindering your service to the Lord.

Until you recognize you are lost without God, destined to spend eternity in hell without His rescuing help, you will never be truly saved.
—Pastor Rod Parsley

No one can touch you like Jesus. He will touch you and change you today if you will let Him. God knows your heart.

The first step to experiencing a personal relationship with Jesus—to receiving Him—is to repent of your sin. Sin separates us from God. Until you recognize you are lost without God, destined to spend eternity in hell without His rescuing help, you will never be truly saved.

Open your heart and get ready right now to receive the outpouring of the priceless Lamb of God. If you want salvation and Jesus Christ to be part of your life, say this simple prayer out loud right now:

> Heavenly Father, I come to you as a sinner, born under sin's curse. I am a child of darkness and of rebellion. I recognize who I am and what I need. I don't just need help. I need salvation! I don't just need to be touched; I need to be recreated.
>
> Lord Jesus Christ, you are the Son of the Living God. Your blood paid the price for my sin. I ask you now to become my Savior. I receive you as my Savior. I take you now as my Redeemer to give me new life, to crush sin's curse, and to make me a new creation.
>
> Satan, I renounce you. You are not my god. I will not serve you. Go from me now!
>
> Lord Jesus Christ, I accept you, believe you, and confess you openly as my personal Savior. Thank you for the price you paid. From this day forward, I intend to serve you as you show me how. Thank you, Lord Jesus.

If you prayed that prayer, you are a brother or sister to millions around the world who know Him as Savior and Lord. Welcome to the family of God! You have the first and most important key to God's protection—a relationship with Him for which you have been destined since the beginning of time. I rejoice with you that you have had the honesty of heart to recognize your need to receive Jesus as personal Savior in your life! Through the coming days, weeks, months, and years, I know God will affirm your salvation and confirm the prayer you have just prayed.

Now that you are one of God's children, you have a new hope! Every situation you face, every circumstance that comes into your life can be victoriously defeated in the name of Jesus.

The Kurku, a hill tribe in India of some 98,000 people, have as their supreme desire and objective in life to be filled with demons. When filled, they believe, their lives will be immune to attack or harm from the evil forces. They believe in God and consider Him a good spirit, though that's faint praise for Someone who created the world and created them. But He does them no harm, so they worship the evil spirits.

What would happen if 98,000 of God's people in this land had as their supreme aim in life to be filled with the Holy Spirit? The Church would awaken, and before very long such a stream of missionaries would go forth so poor souls as the demon worshipers of India might hear of our Savior.

—Student Foreign Missions Fellowship

And when the day of Pentecost was fully come, they were all with one accord in one place. And suddenly there came a sound from heaven as of a rushing mighty wind, and it filled all the house where they were sitting. And there appeared unto them cloven tongues like as of fire, and it sat upon each of them. And they were all filled with the Holy Ghost, and began to speak with other tongues, as the Spirit gave them utterance.

—Acts 2:1-4

It is time to take the Holy Ghost plunge, to get baptized in the Holy Ghost, to get bold in God!

—Pastor Rod Parsley

KEY 2:
BECOME BOLD IN THE HOLY GHOST

Receiving an Acts 2 experience of the baptism in the Holy Ghost is a vital key for God's covering.

It is time for you and me and our born-again brothers and sisters to take the Holy Ghost plunge—to get baptized in the Holy Ghost—to get bold in God! It is time for us to surrender to the moving of the Holy Ghost and to be empowered to withstand Satan's devices in our lives.

It is time to put down your foot, push back your plate, look up to heaven, and say, "I am not going to eat the king's meat. I am going to be like Shadrach, Meschach, and Abednego. I am going to walk through the fiery furnace, but it is not going to touch me. I am going to swim through the flood, but it shall not overflow me. I am going to get baptized in the Holy Ghost."

When you are baptized in the Holy Ghost, you receive power to conquer every circumstance in your life.

The Proof Is in the Pursuit

The proof of your desire for the Holy Spirit in your life is pursuit of Him.

When talking to a friend of mine who plays the piano, I

remarked to him, "I'd sure like to play the piano like you do."

"No, you don't," he immediately replied.

I was taken back by his quick reply, and thinking maybe what I said was not quite clear, I repeated my statement.

Again he replied, "No, you don't."

"Well," I said, a bit frustrated, "what are you talking about?"

"Are you taking lessons?" he asked.

"No."

"Then you are not pursuing what you claim to desire."

He was right. If you desire something, you need to pursue it. The proof of desire is pursuit.

If you want to activate the power of the Holy Ghost in your life and operate in the power of the gifts of the Spirit, then pursue your desire!

When God desired spiritual sons, He sent His only Son, Jesus, down to earth in pursuit of lost souls! When Jesus landed on this earth, He did not just stand back and stare. He came down from heaven, took your sins into His body, and crucified sickness, disease, and sin on Calvary. Then, he rose from the dead, forever defeating the forces of darkness.

When He ascended to heaven, He gave you power to overcome on earth. Before the Ascension, Jesus told the disciples,

> But ye shall receive power, after that the Holy Ghost is come upon you: and ye shall be witnesses unto me both in Jerusalem, and in all Judaea, and in Samaria, and unto the uttermost part of the earth.
> —Acts 1:8

You and I need Holy Ghost power to survive. We need:
• Power to sanctify our tongues.

• Power to live as God instructs us to live.
• Power to cast out devils and speak in new tongues.
• Power to be witnesses for Jesus.
• Power to overcome in the middle of a troubled world, in the midst of perilous times.

Even Jesus received the power of the Holy Ghost. The apostle Peter once preached,

> That word, I say, ye know, which was published throughout all Judaea, and began from Galilee, after the baptism which John preached; How God anointed Jesus of Nazareth with the Holy Ghost and with power: who went about doing good, and healing all that were oppressed of the devil; for God was with him.
>
> —Acts 10:37,38

You cannot fight the devil on your own. Receiving the baptism of the Holy Ghost is a fundamental step in your spiritual survival.

> You do not know what the devil has plotted against you tomorrow, so pray in the Holy Ghost today!
>
> —Pastor Rod Parsley

Prayerlessness is one of the most common sins of our time. Some people who profess to be baptized in the Holy Ghost do not even pray in other tongues five minutes a week. When we fail to pray in tongues, we ignore the power available to us—it's like failing to turn on your furnace in the middle of winter. The apostle Paul wrote,

> For he that speaketh in an unknown tongue speaketh not unto men, but unto God: for no man understandeth him; howbeit in the spirit he speaketh mysteries.
>
> —1 Corinthians 14:2

You pray and speak mysteries. You do not know what you are saying, but God does! When you pray in tongues in Los Angeles, a lady dying of cancer in Kansas City could suddenly takes a turn for the better.

If you do not know how to pray for your teenager who is on drugs and alcohol, pray in the Holy Ghost. If you do not know how to pray for your marriage that is seemingly hopeless, pray in the Holy Ghost. You do not know what the devil has plotted against you tomorrow, so pray in the Holy Ghost today. You do not know what your next financial challenge will be, so pray in the Holy Ghost.

Paul wrote that we don't even have to know what to pray for! The Holy Spirit will even pray for us.

> Likewise the Spirit also helpeth our infirmities: for we know not what we should pray for as we ought: but the Spirit itself maketh intercession for us with groanings which cannot be uttered.
>
> —Romans 8:26

It is time for you and me to experience the covering of God in our lives by walking in the Holy Spirit!

Speaking in tongues is an outward sign of an inward work. When we speak in tongues, we tell the devil, "I am no longer dominated by my mind, my will, or my emotions. My tongue is yielded to the Holy Spirit, even though my mind is void of understanding."

Every time I get on an airplane, I do not know what to pray, so I pray in tongues. Whenever possible, I place my hands on the outside of the plane as I pray. There may be an airplane leaving Los Angeles while I am leaving Atlanta, and the devil may have a plan for them to meet in the air.

But there is Someone inside of me watching over that situation. God knows all about it.

When I begin to pray in the Holy Ghost, I release my God-given power, and I begin to operate in a survival strategy that moves the hand of God on my behalf.

> When you are praying in the Holy Ghost, you are praying mysteries. You are stopping demonic attacks. You are breaking through into the spirit realm.
>
> —Pastor Rod Parsley

One Sunday as I stood in my pulpit, I looked at the camera and said, "I see a man sitting in a hotel room with a cocktail in his hand. You drove there in a white truck with a yellow stripe. You were in the church at one time, but you are not anymore. You are called to ministry. In the name of Jesus, put that cocktail down and give your life to God."

Later, that man called our office and gave us his testimony. Every detail was precise and he gave his life to Jesus as a result of the words I spoke!

Friends, that situation did not occur because of any power that is in Rod Parsley. The power of God through His Holy Spirit created that situation! God had to have that television tape ready at the right time. He had to have that service aired on television at exactly the right moment. He had to stop that man's truck at enough traffic lights to make sure he was in that hotel room when the program hit the air in his city. God orchestrated all of those details to claim that man for His service!

Praying in the Holy Ghost is essential to receive God's covering. Why? When we pray in the Holy Ghost, we are praying mysteries, we are stopping demonic attacks and we are getting through into the spirit realm. The psalmist wrote, "The steps of a good man are ordered by the Lord: and he delighteth in his way" (Psalm 37:23).

Stay prayed up, and God will be able to use you to invade enemy-held territory and bring a mighty deliverance to someone in need. Become personally, intimately acquainted with the third person of the Trinity, who does the work of God in covering His children and protecting them so they can do His work on earth!

I used to think we were automatically led by the Spirit of God because we are the sons of God. In actuality, it is the leading of the Holy Spirit that produces true sonship. Paul described this relationship in one of the most important passages in all of Scripture: "For as many as are led by the Spirit of God, they are the sons of God" (Romans 8:14).

There are two Greek words which translate to the word "sons." "Teknon" means you are a son by right of birth. "Huios" means you are a son because you have adopted the nature of a father through persistent exposure to the nature of that father. "Huios" is the word used in Romans 8:14.

We are not "sons" just because we have been born again. There are many people who are born again who do not have this kind of relationship with God. They are not led by the Spirit of God; they are led by their senses—by what they reason in their mind is right or wrong.

To be led by the Spirit of God, you must know Him—and knowing Him begins with prayer.

The apostle Paul stressed the importance of praying in tongues.

What is it then? I will pray with the spirit, and I will pray with the understanding also: I will sing with the spirit, and I will sing with the understanding also.

—I Corinthians 14:15

He went on to say, "I thank my God, I speak with tongues more than ye all" (v.18).

When we learn to pray in tongues, and to rely on that prayer as our connection with God Almighty, we have used an important key to God's protection.

Having been called to preach the gospel, God forbid that I stoop to be king.

—Charles Haddon Spurgeon

And while they looked stedfastly toward heaven as he went up, behold, two men stood by them in white apparel; Which also said, Ye men of Galilee, why stand ye gazing up into heaven? this same Jesus, which is taken up from you into heaven, shall so come in like manner as ye have seen him go into heaven.

—Acts 1:10,11

When you feel like giving up, keep eternity in front of you, and realize you have come too far to turn back now.

—Pastor Rod Parsley

Key 3:
Never Lose Sight of Eternity

Do you want God's protection? Then you must never lose sight of eternity. The reality of heaven and hell must never be far from your consciousness; it should be a filter through which you make even the most routine decisions. For example, when you see loved ones you know are not in the ark of safety, your first thought should be a vision of them plunging into an eternity in hell.

Heaven is a real place. It is the place where Jesus lives today, and where you and I will live someday. It is mentioned 559 times in the Bible.

All around us, we see evidence of a mindset that declares, "This life is all there is. You might as well go out and enjoy it and satisfy your every need and desire, because when you die, that's it." Even in the church, we often behave as though we do not believe that there is a life beyond this earthly one.

But I'm here to tell you, this life is not forever. It is just a vapor. It is seen, then gone. It is like the grass that grows up and withers. We need to walk in the light of eternity, because we are not going to be here forever.

One pastor in my city has likened our lives to a string between New York and Los Angeles. Our life on earth, he said, is the first millimeter of that string. The rest represents our time in heaven. We'll be there a lot longer than we'll be here!

When you feel like giving up, keep eternity in front of you and realize you have come too far to turn back now. Jesus said,

> Lay not up for yourselves treasures upon earth, where moth and rust doth corrupt, and where thieves break through and steal: But lay up for yourselves treasures in heaven, where neither moth nor rust doth corrupt, and where thieves do not break through nor steal.
>
> —Matthew 6:19,20

When the devil comes in with temptation offering passing pleasure, say, "No, devil, I prefer eternity around the throne of God. My God has prepared a mansion for me." When the enemy tries to put his evil thoughts in your mind, say, "I do not think so, devil; I just do not think so."

Once you've caught sight of heaven—a glimpse of eternity kept ever before you—you can survive the onslaught of hell in these last days. The apostle Paul wrote,

> For if we believe that Jesus died and rose again, even so them also which sleep in Jesus will God bring with him. For this we say unto you by the word of the Lord, that we which are alive and remain unto the coming of the Lord shall not prevent them which are asleep. For the Lord himself shall descend from heaven with a shout, with the voice of the archangel, and with the trump of God: and the dead in Christ shall rise first: Then we which are alive and remain shall be caught up together with them in the clouds, to meet the Lord in the air: and so shall we ever be with the Lord.
>
> —1 Thessalonians 4:14-17

This old ship called 'Zion' has withstood the deadening blows of the God-haters from the foundation of time, and it will continue to do so.

—Pastor Rod Parsley

Jesus said,

But as the days of Noah were, so shall also the coming of the Son of man be.

—Matthew 24:37

God told Noah, "Build me an ark," and He gave Noah the exact blueprint for deliverance.

"Tell the people it is going to rain," God said. "Because of the corruption of the people, I am going to destroy them with a flood." It had never rained before.

In the days of Noah, people were eating and drinking with reckless abandon. They were violating their marriages without a second thought. They were participating in revelry, lawlessness, and lasciviousness. They were out of control, with no restraint.

The creation was separated from the Creator by sin, by agnosticism, and by atheism.

But this old ship called "Zion" has withstood the deadening blows of the God-haters from the foundation of time, and it will continue to do so. As it was in the days of Noah, so it will be today.

And God said unto Noah, The end of all flesh is come before me; for the earth is filled with violence through them; and, behold, I will destroy them with the earth.

—Genesis 6:13

There was a message going out, but it was going unheeded by the people who needed it most. It was a message of warning and deliverance. Only Noah and his house would be saved, because only they had responded to God's instruction.

When the rains began to fall and the ark began to float away, Noah and his family were safe inside. As the flood waters continued to rise, people must have clawed their fingers on the outside of that ark, screaming for deliverance. With water up around their necks, barely able to keep their mouths above water, they almost certainly cried out, "We're drowning; we're dying!"

How strange it would have been in that hour for Noah to have lifted his hands, gathered his family around him like a chorus and begun to sing "The Joy of the Lord," or maybe, "This is the Day," or maybe "Something Good Is Going to Happen to You."

As it was in the days of Noah, so it will be today. How strange it is for men to climb on top of the ark of the anointing of God in the midst of a generation dying in the cesspool of its own self-indulgent sin, and begin to tell them, "Something good is going to happen."

Something good is not going to happen unless we discern the times, realize the day in which we're living, and cry out for God to be merciful to our sin-sick souls.

You must decide which side you're going to play on. You can't be the kicker on the devil's team and the kick returner on God's team.

Make no mistake about it. There will come a time of eternal accountability! Humble yourself and diligently seek God. Keep your eyes on eternity!

In the words of the prophet,

Behold, the day of the Lord cometh, cruel both with wrath and fierce anger, to lay the land desolate:

and he shall destroy the sinners thereof out of it. For the stars of heaven and the constellations thereof shall not give their light: the sun shall be darkened in his going forth, and the moon shall not cause her light to shine. And I will punish the world for their evil, and the wicked for their iniquity; and I will cause the arrogancy of the proud to cease, and will lay low the haughtiness of the terrible. . . .Every one that is found shall be thrust through; and every one that is joined unto them shall fall by the sword.

—Isaiah 13:9-11, 15

Ask the Holy Spirit to help you stay humble and contrite before God, whose name is holy! With your eyes focused on Him, you will soon (after the vapor of this life is over) dwell with Him in that "high and holy place."

Eternal vigilance is the price of freedom.
—Thomas Payne

Be sober, be vigilant; because your adversary the devil, as a roaring lion, walketh about, seeking whom he may devour.
—1 Peter 5:8

We must be vigilant and watchful. We must wake up spiritually and stay alert!
—Pastor Rod Parsley

KEY 4:
BE VIGILANT

You and I must be vigilant to remain under God's covering. Too many of us run down to an altar, have some preacher tap us on the head with a little bit of oil, and expect every satanic assault will be stopped for the rest of our lives. It is not going to happen that way.

We must wake up and be vigilant over our lives and our homes. To do that, we must be watchful for the enemy. We must learn to recognize danger signs. The apostle Paul wrote, "For if the trumpet give an uncertain sound, who shall prepare himself to the battle" (1 Corinthians 14:8)?

Sodom and Gomorrah perished because the residents of those cities were not vigilant. They did not recognize the enemy of corruption that deceived them into partaking in sinful pleasures.

Centuries later, those cities remained a warning to the early church. Jude wrote,

> Even as Sodom and Gomorrha, and the cities about them in like manner, giving themselves over to fornication, and going after strange flesh, are set forth for an example, suffering the vengeance of eternal fire.
>
> —Jude 7

The devil is plotting and planning your demise. Right now, he is scheming to get you into a position of vulnerability—out from under the cover of the protection of God. He's planning right now. He has a strategy. And he has all the time in the world—he's a spirit being; he doesn't need to sleep.

Call upon the protection of God Almighty. Speak the Word of God over your family and declare, "Devil, you're not having my teenager." When your children get ready for school, raise up a prayer cover over them that day so no bully, drug dealer, or pornography peddler can corrupt your child. The apostle Paul wrote,

> For when they shall say, Peace and safety; then sudden destruction cometh upon them, as travail upon a woman with child; and they shall not escape.
> —1 Thessalonians 5:3

When is the last time you rebuked the spirit of divorce from your home? Gather your family together and sanctify your home unto God. Determine that nothing unholy, untrue, or impure will cross the threshold of your home. As Paul counseled the church at Corinth, "Wherefore let him that thinketh he standeth take heed lest he fall" (1 Corinthians 10:12).

> We draw our strength from the battle. Our greatest conflicts come from our greatest victories!
> —Pastor Rod Parsley

It is time for us to realize that in Satan, we have an adversary who means business. Jesus said,

> The thief cometh not, but for to steal, and to kill, and to destroy: I am come that they might have life,

and that they might have it more abundantly.

—John 10:10

The devil desires to stop us any way he can. You and I need to be receptive and responsive to the Word of God concerning the strategies of our adversary. We must understand how he works, and be vigilant to know his ways.

As Solomon declared, along with a season for all other activities under the sun, there is "a time to love, and a time to hate; a time of war, and a time of peace" (Ecclesiastes 3:8).

We are in a war, declared by the devil. So we need to be vigilant. Satan does not rest. He wants to destroy you and your family.

Jesus, on the other hand, came to give us rest. He said,

Peace I leave with you, my peace I give unto you: not as the world giveth, give I unto you. Let not your heart be troubled, neither let it be afraid.

—John 14:27

We Christians today spend a lot of time looking for peace. We do not want anything to disturb us. We want everything to be comfortable, but we do not want to maintain vigilance. Our nation's military history has taught us that sometimes, a war has to come before true peace can exist. That is how it is with our battles with the devil. If we want true peace, we must not shy away from fighting the war in which he has already engaged us.

Christianity is meant to be more difficult than the other lifestyles we could choose. So why do we so often think it's all right to just go to church, come back on Sunday night, sing and dance, go home and go to bed—and never raise up a prayer cover? That is not fighting the war the devil has engaged us in. That is not being vigilant.

Every night, I pray along these lines before I go to bed: "Father, into your hands I commend my mind. No force from without may attack my mind while I sleep. My mind will think only thoughts of blessing. Father, if there's anything that comes to my mind, it must be sifted through the filter of the Holy Ghost and the Word of God. Right now, I raise up a prayer cover over my mind."

Then I lay hands on my children and pray over them with words similar to these: "These children will sleep in the safety and peace of the covering of prayer that surrounds them. No force from the supernatural sphere, no principality, no power, no strategy, no design, no desire of the enemy can penetrate the cover of prayer I raise over them now, in Jesus' name."

That is engaging the battle against the devil. And with Almighty God fighting alongside us, our victory is assured!

> It is time we circled the wagons, pulled out the
> artillery, rolled up our sleeves, and readied ourselves
> to be tough with the devil.
> —Pastor Rod Parsley

You and I need to stop romanticizing our battle with the evil one. The devil is not a little man in a red suit with a pitchfork and horns. He is Satan—the thief, the master deceiver, the murderer! He is behind every heinous crime ever committed, and he will damn your soul to hell if you let him. He will rape your family, steal your finances, and leave you on the trash heap of wreck and ruin—if you let him.

The devil hates you. He wants preachers fighting with preachers. He wants Christians fighting with Christians. He will do anything he can to destroy us.

He will sit a person delivered from alcoholism on an airplane and have a stewardess offer him a drink. He will place a recovering drug addict in a hotel room next door to a room thick with marijuana smoke. He will take a man who is struggling with sexual temptation, and arrange for him to work with an attractive, flirtatious woman.

He will get you if he can. And he isn't bound by conscience, so he will do whatever it takes to snare you.

This is your wake-up alarm!

We are in a spiritual battlefield, not a heavenly recreation room. We are facing the very forces of hell. Understand right now that the devil is out to stop you. Get this settled in your spirit. Call on the covering of God against the schemes of the adversary. It is time to get serious if we are going to survive.

For as many as are led by the Spirit of God, they
are the sons of God.

—Romans 8:14

It's time to call upon God's covering with regard
to our spirit lives. We can start by understanding that
we are spirit beings!

—Pastor Rod Parsley

KEY 5:
STAY TUNED TO THE SPIRIT

When you are born again, you are born of the Spirit. There's something inside you greater than what is wrapped around you.

We are spirit beings. Our bodies are just packaging. We have been born of the eternal Word of God, and that seed remains in us. We are eternal, invincible, and indestructible.

You say, "Not so. I could take out a gun and shoot you in the head, and you'd die." Yes, my body would die. But what makes me me would still be alive. And it would be waiting for you to join me in heaven.

We do have a struggle; it is the battle of the ages—but you can survive this battle. To survive, you need to:

• Get in touch with that part of you that's born of God; and

• Get in tune with your spirit.

The Bible says the spirit of a man shall sustain all his infirmities—including the weakness of his flesh. That's the reason I do not believe born again people who say "The devil made me do it. I was weak. I fell into sin."

That is impossible. You cannot fall into sin. The Bible plainly says, "He maketh my feet like hinds' feet, and setteth me upon my high places" (Psalm 18:33).

When we become born again, our new nature is one that desires to stay away from sin.

It's time to call upon God's covering with regard to our spirit lives. We can begin by understanding that we are spirit beings! The spirit being in most Christians is emaciated. In the spirit realm, they are like starving refugees, little tiny beings with knees bigger than their thighs.

Your natural man wakes up and says, "It's breakfast time," and at noon, "It's lunch time," and in the evening, "It's supper time," and every hour in between, "It's snack time."

But many don't even look at their Bibles outside church service. Just like the natural man eats natural food to live, the spirit man must receive spiritual food to live.

To stay in tune in the spirit, you have to feed your spirit. And your spirit lives by faith. Scripture is full of teaching about faith.

Galatians 3:11 tells us, "But that no man is justified by the law in the sight of God, it is evident: for, The just shall live by faith."

Hebrews 11:1 admonishes us, "Now faith is the substance of things hoped for, the evidence of things not seen."

If you're going to know the benefits of God's protection in perilous times, you need to have a faith that knows. You need to have a faith that grows. You need to have a faith that's rooted.

Faith is the conduit from heaven to earth. It is the sixth sense God gives you. The hand of faith reaches into the realm of the spirit and pulls whatever you need into the natural.

A natural man is born by the joining together of the seed of the man and egg of the woman. That egg is alive, but it's abiding in a state of death. If it is not touched by the seed of the man, it will be cast off.

When the seed of the man touches the egg of the woman, conception takes place. Conception is the joining of that which is without to that which is within, producing a new offspring.

We have the same hope the egg of that woman has. The only way for it to live is to receive something in itself from without. Something outside has to get in, and that something is the incorruptible seed of the Word of God.

That Word can't get planted in your mind; it will die there. It's like the seed sown on stony ground in Jesus' parable. The sun comes up and bakes it dry because it has no root. When a trial comes your way, you give up on God because all you have is mental assent. You don't have firm roots to draw on God's nourishment.

You and I must be born of the Spirit. That's the reason the Bible indicates that the things of the spirit are enmity to the carnal mind. The apostle Paul wrote,

> For to be carnally minded is death; but to be spiritually minded is life and peace. Because the carnal mind is enmity against God: for it is not subject to the law of God, neither indeed can be.
>
> —Romans 8:6,7

If you are living in the flesh, or allowing your old sin nature to influence you, you cannot please God. Feed your spirit with the Word of God. Keep your spirit strong with the Word of God to survive the attacks of the devil. Unless you learn to be led by your spirit, you will follow the dictates of your mind, and you will follow the dictates of your flesh. Paul continued,

> So then they that are in the flesh cannot please God. But ye are not in the flesh, but in the Spirit, if so be that the Spirit of God dwell in you. Now if any

man have not the Spirit of Christ, he is none of his. And if Christ be in you, the body is dead because of sin; but the Spirit is life because of righteousness.

—Romans 8:8-10

If you are led by the Spirit, if you're in tune to the Spirit, your body is reckoned dead. Being dead has some significant advantages! For instance, a dead body cannot be tempted.

When we are reckoned dead, the Spirit of God dwells in us, deadening the appetites of the flesh and soul as we give Him expression in our lives. As we allow the Spirit to dwell in us moment by moment, day by day, week after week, year after year, it is continually separating us and setting us apart for His service, a process known as sanctification.

Yet far too often, we are not tuned in to the Holy Spirit. We do not give the Spirit an opportunity to express His nature. We are not letting God sanctify us. God is telling us, "Hey, you don't owe your flesh anything!" When it cries out, "You owe me a piece of coconut cream pie," or when it cries out, "I want to be sick" —remember, you can overcome temptation if you are in tune with your spirit.

When you and I overcome temptation, the devil will tuck his tail and run (he's a coward at heart). So feed your spirit with the Word of God. Get in touch with that life on the inside of you.

You can base your life on who God is, what God is, and what God says.

—Pastor Rod Parsley

God is accurate in His communication with us. By staying in tune with the Holy Spirit we learn to be "accurate." His Spirit keeps us "on target" to those things He wants for our life.

Malachi is the last book of the Old Covenant, and I have always found last words very interesting. Malachi is God's last statement before 400 years of silence. If you were not going to talk again for 400 years, the last thing you had to say would be very significant.

God said,

> And I will come near to you to judgment; and I will be a swift witness against the sorcerers, and against the adulterers, and against false swearers, and against those that oppress the hireling in his wages, the widow, and the fatherless, and that turn aside the stranger from his right, and fear not me, saith the Lord of hosts. For I am the Lord, I change not; therefore ye sons of Jacob are not consumed.
>
> —Malachi 3:5,6

God's laws and covenants never change. Your spiritual target is always the same, and you will never miss it if your spirit is strong.

Who God is, what He is, and what He says never changes. But today, many Christians want to change God. They want Him to conform to their own idolatrous image of who they think He is. They pray for God's help to accomplish what they have already decided to do, instead of seeking God's will for their lives. They want to form a molten calf, a graven image on the inside of their own hearts, of a God that fits into their own lifestyle.

God won't fool around with that kind of attitude. He will step right in the middle of that scenario and say, "Hold on. Wait just a minute. It does not matter what you think about your situation; I will never change. It does not matter how you try to mold me; I will never change. It does not matter what men say about me, or what philosophy says, or what contemporary religion says. I will never change." The author of Hebrews told us,

> Jesus Christ the same yesterday, and to day, and for ever. Be not carried about with divers and strange doctrines. For it is a good thing that the heart be established with grace; not with meats, which have not profited them that have been occupied therein.
>
> —Hebrews 13:8,9

You can base your life on who God is, what God is, and what God says. It is the only sure thing in this world. Who would have guessed that the towers of the World Trade Center would not always be part of the Manhattan skyline? That hole in the sky is a stark reminder that anything on this earth can change. The only stability in this whole universe is: God will never change.

Keep your eye on the mark, and you will hit the spiritual target every single time! The apostle Paul wrote,

> I press toward the mark for the prize of the high calling of God in Christ Jesus. Let us therefore, as many as be perfect, be thus minded: and if in any thing ye be otherwise minded, God shall reveal even this unto you.
>
> —Philippians 3:14,15

Paul was saying, "I have my spiritual target clearly in my spirit, and it is to be like Jesus Christ. And if my mind ever starts to veer from that target, I rely on the Holy Spirit to reveal to me the error of my way." If our lives are to be steadfast, we must do as Paul did. We must walk in tune with the Holy Spirit that reflects God's truth.

I never want to hear it said I have to die and cannot live; therefore, I get up in the morning and I am
watchful.

—Pastor Rod Parsley

Stay in tune with your Heavenly Father through the Holy
Spirit, and you will know when the adversary attempts to
attack you and your family.

You say, "I do not know how this cancer got in my
body." Wake up! The devil had a plan, and you did not do
anything to counteract it.

Often, I wake up in the morning and say, "Thank you.
God, for healing me of cancer."

"You have never had cancer," you say.

That is exactly my point—I have never had it, and I do
not ever intend to have it! I never want to hear said I have to
die and cannot live; therefore, I get up in the morning and I
am watchful. I ask the Holy Spirit to keep me in tune with
His holy will for my life.

I say, "Devil, no cancer cell can live in my body. If while
I was asleep it began to invade my body, it has to leave now,
in the name of Jesus. My bloodstream is cleansed; my mind
is alert; my bones and tissues function properly; my heart is
strong; my lungs are strong."

What am I doing? I am watching and staying on target
with the spiritual realities in my life. I am deflecting fiery
darts with the powerful shield of faith Paul referred to in
Ephesians 6:16: "Above all, taking the shield of faith, wherewith ye shall be able to quench all the fiery darts of the
wicked."

If I am watchful, walking in tune with the Holy Spirit, I
will survive hell's onslaught in these last days.

You get involved in hope beyond the scope of

natural human limitation when you begin to pray in the Holy Ghost.

—Pastor Rod Parsley

You are born of the Spirit. In Romans, Paul recorded this promise: "For as many as are led by the Spirit of God, they are the sons of God" (Romans 8:14).

When you are led by the Spirit, you have God's covering protection. You can traverse the storms of life—the perils of perilous times—and come out on the other side.

Your clothes will not smell like smoke even though you go through the fire. The Holy Spirit knows how to get us through the treacherous fires and furnaces set ablaze by the enemy.

As we operate in the spiritual realm, looking to Jesus as our guide, we have authority to command demon power to release every hold on us, on our families, and our lives. We should not be afraid to exercise the authority that God has clearly given us in Scripture.

Learn to pray in the Holy Ghost for the perfect will of the Father to be accomplished in your life.

Do not blame your inconsistencies on God. He has never failed. He has never lost a battle. You are in a kingdom that cannot be shaken.

—Pastor Rod Parsley

God has given us His gifts to help keep us accurate in our spiritual walk. His Spirit helps us flow in His will. The apostle Paul wrote,

But the manifestation of the Spirit is given to every man to profit withal. For to one is given by the Spirit the word of wisdom; to another the word of knowledge by the same Spirit; To another faith by the same Spirit; to another the gifts of healing by the same Spirit; To another the working of miracles; to another prophecy; to another discerning of spirits; to another divers kinds of tongues; to another the inter-pretation of tongues.

—1 Corinthians 12:7-10

We need to understand everything we can about the gifts that God has given to His children. If you do not understand the gifts of the Spirit, how will they operate in your life?

If spiritual gifts are not working in your life, will you fall apart when trials come to you? Will you run out of the king-dom of God, saying these gifts do not work? You could, but you'd be wrong. If you do not know how to do algebra, you do not run around saying "Algebra does not work." Instead, you would say, "I do not know how to do algebra."

Do not blame your inconsistencies on God. He has never failed. He has never lost a battle. He is so accurate that He never misses the mark!

You are in a kingdom that cannot be shaken. The psalmist wrote, "In the multitude of my thoughts within me thy comforts delight my soul" (Psalm 94:19).

Did you ever have a time when it just seemed like every-thing was going wrong, and your anxious thoughts were multiplied within you? Then be honest with God. He can handle it! And He welcomes the prayers of His children who seek hard after Him.

You and I have hope beyond the borders of human limi-tation. God and His Word are not bound. You may be bound, but the Word of God is not bound, and it shall give you life. Jesus gave His life for you so that you might walk in salva-tion and life. He said,

No man taketh [my life] from me, but I lay it down of myself. I have power to lay it down, and I have power to take it again. This commandment have I received of my Father.

—John 10:18

In His life on earth, Jesus was swung up on a cross, hung between heaven and hell, looking like a sacrificial animal. When they took Him from the cross, they brushed His blood-soaked, matted hair. They wrapped Him in grave clothes, put Him in the borrowed tomb of Joseph of Arimathaea, and rolled a stone in front of the burial place. The hopes and dreams of the disciples were shattered.

But praise God, that isn't where the story ends! Jesus rose triumphant over death, dwelled among us, and ascended into heaven. Then He sent the Holy Spirit so we would not have to live without His power. The living Word of God is inside you today in the form of the Holy Spirit.

We have the covering protection of Almighty God in these perilous times because He is there to guide us, to keep us on target, to keep us pressing forward toward the mark in all things.

No circumstances can hold us or keep us down as we press forward toward the high calling. With the apostle Paul we can say, "I press toward the mark for the prize of the high calling of God in Christ Jesus" (Philippians 3:14).

Jesus—the living Word—broke through apparent defeat into glorious victory. Stay tuned to the Holy Spirit, and trust Him to bring you safely through!

Someone has taken the time to review the history of war and learned that in the last 4,000 years, there have been but 268 years entirely free from war. This, of course, only takes into consideration 'man's inhumanity to man;' for if man's inhumanity to God were to be considered, it would have to be said there has not been a single moment from the fall of man to the present minute that has been entirely free from war.

—Gospel Herald

Ye shall not need to fight in this battle: set yourselves, stand ye still, and see the salvation of the Lord with you, O Judah and Jerusalem: fear not, nor be dismayed; to morrow go out against them: for the Lord will be with you.

—2 Chronicles 20:17

Do not write letters to our men of God saying, 'I am deeply sorry you fell.' Instead, write them letters that say, 'I am sorry I let go.

—Pastor Rod Parsley

KEY 6:
REALIZE SPIRITUAL WARFARE IS THE WAR

All twelve disciples had the joy of walking and talking with Jesus while He lived on the face of this earth. He loved them, and they loved Him.

Matthew was a tax collector, but he gave up his profession to follow Jesus. John was a fisherman, but he gave up his fishing business to follow Jesus.

Yet, Jesus said specifically to Peter, "Simon, Simon, behold, Satan hath desired to have you, that he may sift you as wheat" (Luke 22:31).

Jesus was serious about His mission, and He understood the nature of the enemy. The devil did not have his eyes focused on Matthew or John. Jesus said, "Simon, Satan has desired to have you," because Jesus understood that Satan wanted to attack the man who would be indispensable to the birth of the church. Peter was a church leader, so he was a prime target for the forces of hell! Can we expect that 2,000 years later, Satan would abandon that strategy?

I recently heard someone say, "Well, it disturbs me that there have been so many so-called church leaders who have fallen into sin." And it should be disturbing! Friend, this is spiritual warfare.

But let us put the responsibility where it belongs: these leaders have not fallen as much as we have dropped them!

71

The Bible says,

> Confess your faults one to another, and pray one
> for another, that ye may be healed. The effectual fer-
> vent prayer of a righteous man availeth much.
> —James 5:16

If the body of Christ had been serious about the church
and about its leaders, then we would have been praying
earnestly for God to protect them, just as Jesus prayed
earnestly for protection upon Peter.

Jesus knew the importance of prayer. In the Garden of
Gethsemane, He revealed to His disciples this vital key to
God's protection. Jesus was facing the greatest battle of His
life as He looked toward the suffering, shame, and death of
the cross. He went up to the Mount of Olives to pray. He
knew He needed to be strengthened in prayer. He knew He
needed spiritual energy to face what was before Him.

Before He entered into a time of prayer and travail
before God, He told His disciples, "Pray that ye enter not
into temptation" (Luke 22:40).

You know the rest of the story. The apostles fell asleep.
Today, I believe we often are spiritually asleep, not realizing
that Satan is lurking just around the corner, ready to attack us
and our spiritual leaders at any moment. It is up to us to support those leaders in prayer.

It may be that our spiritual leaders have not fallen.
Perhaps we have dropped them from our prayer petitions to
God Almighty!

Do not become caught up on the bandwagon of bashing
preachers and believers. Do not turn your spiritual machine
gun on the very people fighting with you in the same Army
of God. It is time to quit killing our wounded, and begin
extending our support to our wounded foxhole buddies.

We need the foot soldiers as well as the generals if we are to defeat the enemy.

"Well, Pastor Rod," you reply, "that is easy for you to say. But the simple fact is there are many who have fallen from grace who did not do everything just right." And that may be true. But do you do everything just right? As Jesus said, "He that is without sin among you, let him first cast a stone at her" (John 8:7).

When no one was willing to stone the woman who was in adultery, Jesus asked her, "Woman, where are those thine accusers? hath no man condemned thee? She said, No man, Lord. And Jesus said unto her, Neither do I condemn thee: go, and sin no more" (John 8:10,11).

I see the broken lives of believers all around me, but I do not—and cannot—place the blame on them. Instead, the Holy Spirit leads me to pray, "God, help me hold on tighter. Let me take hold of the horns of the altar; let me thwart every satanic opposition against their lives, in the name of Jesus."

A great general once said, "War is hell." In the realm of the spirit, his words are only too true. Our war is literally against hell and all it stands for; and we must not ever forget it.

You and I need to pray for those who have fallen. Ask God to be merciful in His judgment, and to restore them to His grace. Remember, God's judgment is far fairer than any we can impose, and it is a judgment to be feared by those who refuse to walk in His precepts.

The author of Hebrews wrote,

> He that despised Moses' law died without mercy under two or three witnesses: Of how much sorer punishment, suppose ye, shall he be thought worthy, who hath trodden under foot the Son of God, and hath counted the blood of the covenant, wherewith

he was sanctified, an unholy thing, and hath done despite unto the Spirit of grace? For we know him that hath said, Vengeance belongeth unto me, I will recompense, saith the Lord. And again, The Lord shall judge his people. It is a fearful thing to fall into the hands of the living God.

—Hebrews 10:28-31

Our leaders need God's covering through our prayers. Let's be intentional about giving His protection to them!

The quality of a person's life is in direct proportion to their commitment to excellence, regardless of their chosen field of endeavor.

—Coach Vince Lombardi

Nothing in the world can take the place of persistence. Talent will not; nothing is more common than unsuccessful men with talent. Genius will not; unrewarded genius is almost a proverb. Education will not; the world is full of educated derelicts. Persistence and determination are omnipotent.

—President Calvin Coolidge

Wherefore take unto you the whole armour of God, that ye may be able to withstand in the evil day, and having done all, to stand. Stand therefore, having your loins girt about with truth, and having on the breastplate of righteousness; And your feet shod with the preparation of the gospel of peace; Above all, taking the shield of faith, wherewith ye shall be able to quench all the fiery darts of the wicked. And take the helmet of salvation, and the sword of the Spirit, which is the word of God.

—Ephesians 6:13-17

Samson had anointed power for spiritual battle as long as he lived within his covenant. Even when no other weapon was available, he was able to use the jawbone of an ass to slay his enemies.

—Pastor Rod Parsley

KEY 7:
LEARN YOUR WEAPONS

The first rule in developing skill with the weapons of the Spirit is to use what is familiar. The level of your protection will not be determined by how extensive your spiritual tool box is, but by your ability to use the tools available to you.

David tried on Saul's armor, but said, "Thanks, but no thanks. I am sure it is good armor, but is not comfortable for me. By the way, Saul, this armor has not done much for you lately, either." (See 1 Samuel 17:39.)

Instead of using Saul's armor, David chose his own weapon—weapon that had been tried in the heat of battle. David took with him a familiar weapon. He had "proven" his sling. He had killed a lion and a bear with it. David understood what his sling could do, and he fully understood the power of the God he served.

> Then said David to the Philistine, Thou comest to me with a sword, and with a spear, and with a shield: but I come to thee in the name of the Lord of hosts, the God of the armies of Israel, whom thou hast defied.
>
> —I Samuel 17:45

David knew he had the right weapon, and he was ready

to use it. More importantly, David knew he had the right God —the very Lord of hosts, and he was ready to serve Him!

The second rule in learning how to properly use your spiritual weapons is to develop your spiritual strength. No matter how skillful a soldier is with his weapon, an exhausted 98-pound weakling cannot defeat a stronger foe over the long course of battle.

You need constant and continual spiritual exercise to build and maintain your strength! The author of Hebrews wrote,

> But strong meat belongeth to them that are of full age, even those who by reason of use have their senses exercised to discern both good and evil.
> —Hebrews 5:14

Do you see it? The strong get that way by exercise, by "reason of use." God has given us spiritual senses to discern the enemy and discern your fellow warriors. We need to exercise those senses if we want them to be useful to us.

If you have the power of God's anointing on your life, you can defeat the devil by learning how to use the spiritual weapons He has given you, and by exercising your spirit man to stay fit for battle.

Samson had anointed power for battle. Even when no other weapon was available, he was able to use the jawbone of an ass to slay his enemies.

> And he found a new jawbone of an ass, and put forth his hand, and took it, and slew a thousand men therewith.
> —Judges 15:15

The third rule in using spiritual weapons is to live within your covenant. Samson had power as long as he lived within his covenant. When he strayed from his covenant, he lost his power.

We need to understand that no matter how skillful we become with our weapons, the true source of our strength is not in that skill. Our power comes from personal holiness and our developing relationship to God. Our faithfulness to His covenant determines the amount of power we have available to us. The Bible says,

> For this is the covenant that I will make with the house of Israel after those days, saith the Lord; I will put my laws into their mind, and write them in their hearts: and I will be to them a God, and they shall be to me a people.
>
> —Hebrews 8:10

Saul was skillful with a sword and spear. But because he was out of covenant with God, Goliath humiliated him.

Goliath had a valiant war record. But as an uncircumcised Philistine, he was not in covenant with God. David understood his covenant relationship, and triumphed.

When we understand our covenant relationship with God, He will cover us with the power to face even the most daunting of perils. As the author of Hebrews tells us,

> Let us draw near with a true heart in full assurance of faith, having our hearts sprinkled from an evil conscience, and our bodies washed with pure water. Let us hold fast the profession of our faith without wavering; (for he is faithful that promised;) And let us consider one another to provoke unto love and to good works.
>
> —Hebrews 10:22-24

Purity and a true heart are the spiritual keys to unlocking

the power of God in your life. You and I must have faith that He will stand by our sides, no matter what the battle. If we are faithful and obedient, He will cover us according to the promises in His loving covenant.

> The Bible doesn't say 'if the enemy comes in;' it says 'when the enemy comes in.' I am getting ready for the onslaughts of hell.
> —Pastor Rod Parsley

Years ago, an evangelistic power-lifting team came to minister at our church. Early in the day, I saw them walking around with bowls of food in their hands. I said, "What do you have in the bowls?"

They showed me—boiled spaghetti with nothing on it, boiled potatoes with nothing on them. And they had big chunks of bread.

They would grab a potato, then they would grab some spaghetti, then they would start in on the bread. They ate it all.

Eating that bland diet was part of the price they paid to be weight lifters. Watching them, I suddenly realized, "That is what I must look like in the spirit!"

I read the Word God for my spiritual nourishment. It provides me with the energy I need to get through the day. Do I need the nourishment right this second? No, but I am storing it up.

I am getting ready for the onslaughts of hell. When those onslaughts come, I will have the power to defeat every adversary because I was faithful to feed my spirit man.

You are a spirit. And that spirit man needs to be fed!

We know our bodies need to be fed, and we carefully plan our meals when we shop for our food. At the store, we think, "I will buy some of these spices, because next

Thursday I am going to have hot chicken wings. And on Friday, I am going to have roast beef. And then, I better not buy anything for Saturday night, because that is when we go out for pizza. On next Monday, I think I will prepare chicken and a green salad."

We typically do a good job of planning how we will nourish our physical bodies. Why should we be haphazard about the way we nourish our spiritual bodies? We should apply the same methodical approach we use at the grocery store to how we feed our spirits. There is a spiritual assault coming from the corridors of hell, and you need to learn how to feed your spirit man. You need to fortify yourself with strong spiritual ammunition.

Get ready! Feed your spirit man by abiding in the shadow of the Almighty. As the psalmist wrote,

> He that dwelleth in the secret place of the most High shall abide under the shadow of the Almighty. I will say of the Lord, He is my refuge and my fortress: my God; in him will I trust. Surely he shall deliver thee from the snare of the fowler, and from the noisome pestilence.
>
> —Psalm 91:1-3

To feed your spirit man, study the Word of God. Memorize it. Let it sink deep into your spirit. It is the most tangible and powerful weapon God has given us for our spiritual arsenal. We are promised in the Bible of the Word's power:

> For the word of God is quick, and powerful, and sharper than any twoedged sword, piercing even to the dividing asunder of soul and spirit, and of the

joints and marrow, and is a discerner of the thoughts
and intents of the heart.

—Hebrews 4:12

I believe we are heading toward the imminent
return of the King of kings and the Lord of lords. I
believe Jesus is coming.

—Pastor Rod Parsley

The spiritual warfare of these last days involves all the
weapons and all the armaments of the spirit. I believe we are
living in the last hours of the last days. Jesus said, "But of
that day and hour knoweth no man, no, not the angels of
heaven, but my Father only" (Matthew 24:36).

Jesus said that even though we would not know the day
and hour of His return, we would know the season. I pray
you understand the relevance and urgency of the message
that God has deposited in my spirit for this end-time season.
It is time to get ready! Something is about to happen.

I believe those chariots that have not ridden the wind
since the days of Elijah are being polished by the heavenly
hosts and will soon be pulled out of their stalls.

I believe we are heading toward the imminent return of
our Lord and Savior, Jesus Christ, and I believe He is coming soon.

It is time for today's church to become like the glorious
church of Ephesus. Jesus gave the apostle John lavish words
of praise for that church:

Unto the angel of the church of Ephesus write;
These things saith he that holdeth the seven stars in
his right hand, who walketh in the midst of the seven
golden candlesticks; I know thy works, and thy
labour, and thy patience, and how thou canst not

bear them which are evil: and thou hast tried them which say they are apostles, and are not, and hast found them liars: And hast borne, and hast patience, and for my name's sake hast laboured, and hast not fainted.

—Revelation 2:1-3

I pray that the worldwide body of Christ will learn to mirror the church of Ephesus, and recognize we are in a spiritual war. As we fight this war, I pray God will see that we are strong, and that even in the heaviest attacks of the enemies, we do not faint!

"Well, we are in the middle of revival," some Christians say, "and there is a great outpouring." Yet, other Christians claim, "This is one of the coldest, darkest days ever in the history of the church. We are a dead church in the middle of a dying world." Which is it?

A close examination of the Word of God will reveal that as Christ's return approaches, the cold will get colder and the hot will get hotter.

There is going to be a verifiable polarization of the kingdom of darkness and the kingdom of Light. You are going to walk in one kingdom or the other—so walk in the light.

As we draw close to God and spend time in His presence, we take on His radiance and character.

—Pastor Rod Parsley

Submit yourselves therefore to God. Resist the devil, and he will flee from you. Draw nigh to God, and he will draw nigh to you. Cleanse your hands, ye sinners; and purify your hearts, ye double minded.

—James 4:7,8

KEY 8:
LIVE IN GOD'S RADIANCE

There is a story told of a man with a beautiful wife and a three-year-old daughter. Sudden sorrow struck the home when the young wife was killed in a traffic accident, and it seemed that all of the light had gone out of the man's life forever.

The night after the funeral, the young father was putting his daughter to bed, when the lights suddenly went out all over the house. He suspected that a fuse had blown out in the basement, and said to the girl, "Papa will be right back; you lie still and wait here."

But the girl, frightened at the thought of being left alone, pleaded to be taken with him, so he picked her up in his arms and started through the darkened hallway and down the stairs. The girl snuggled in her father's arms for a while in silence; but as they entered the basement she tightened her arms about his neck, and said, "It is awfully dark; but I am not afraid, because my papa is here!"

A sob shook the man's whole body. He buried his face in the baby's hair and wept, as he said, "Yes, dear, it is dark, indeed; but I also am not afraid because my Father is here!"

Drawing close to God—deliberately seeking His covering and protection—is essential to making the devil flee from you.

Moses spent time with God, and the very holiness of God so permeated his face it actually radiated the glory of the Almighty! The Bible says,

> And the children of Israel saw the face of Moses, that the skin of Moses' face shone: and Moses put the vail upon his face again, until he went in to speak with him.
>
> —Exodus 34:35

Jesus was the express image, the living radiance of the Father:

> Who being the brightness of his glory, and the express image of his person, and upholding all things by the word of his power, when he had by himself purged our sins, sat down on the right hand of the Majesty on high.
>
> —Hebrews 1:3

The word "image" in this Scripture comes from the Greek word "charakter" and means "character." This was a term used in making coins. A metal disk, usually gold or silver, was heated in a hot flame. The desired mold or image was then placed over it and struck with a hammer. This striking process placed the image on the mold deep into the softened metal disk.

We see three things here:

• First, to become His express image, to draw near to our Holy God, we must be heated by the fire. This is either in the heat of the glory of His presence or in the heat of adversity and persecution. Christians could avoid a lot of adversity if they would allow their lives to be softened in the heat of His glory. But one way or the other, by glory or by adversity, we will have to be softened if we are to take on His image. The apostle Paul, no stranger to suffering, wrote, "Yea, and all that will live godly in Christ Jesus shall suffer persecution" (2 Timothy 3:12).

• Two, to become His express image—no matter how soft or yielded we are—we must come into personal and intimate contact with Him to receive His image. God wants us to be in a close relationship with Him. Jesus said,

> I am the good shepherd: the good shepherd giveth his life for the sheep. But he that is an hireling, and not the shepherd, whose own the sheep are not, seeth the wolf coming, and leaveth the sheep, and fleeth: and the wolf catcheth them, and scattereth the sheep. The hireling fleeth, because he is an hireling, and careth not for the sheep. I am the good shepherd, and know my sheep, and am known of mine.
>
> —John 10:11-14

If we do not have a personal relationship with God, when the wolf (the devil) comes, we will flee in fear. But if we know God, we will have the strength to defeat Satan in our daily battles.

• Three, there will be a striking process where the character of God is branded into our spirits. It may come as a shock to you, but while resting in Jesus' arms, you might suddenly experience a sharp spiritual blow that will drive you so close to Jesus that His image is stamped permanently upon you. That stamp allows you to receive His mind and His love. His wisdom and His glory. The apostle Paul wrote,

> But we all, with open face beholding as in a
> glass the glory of the Lord, are changed into the
> same image from glory to glory, even as by the
> Spirit of the Lord.
>
> —2 Corinthians 3:18

To be holy and to survive in this season of devastation
and doom, we must be sealed in the sanctity of God through
His Holy Spirit.

> In the midst of the trials of life, it is one thing to
> know God as Deliverer, Helper, Comforter. It is
> another thing to have God say, "I know this man."
>
> —Pastor Rod Parsley

I shared with you earlier how the devil will especially
attack men like Peter—men who are chosen by God to be
His spiritual leaders. But he won't stop there. The devil will
also attack any Christian serving God. In these times of personal attack, it is essential to stay close to God, obey His precepts, and bask in His holiness and power.

Once a former music minister of mine left his home to
begin his day's tasks, as many of us do each day. Although
he never wears a seat belt, he felt something telling him to
put it on that day. Later, he was involved in an accident that
would have sent him through the windshield of his car and
into the windshield of the other car had he not been wearing
his seat belt. He is alive today and serving God because he
obeyed that "something." The police officer said he surely
would have been dead at the scene if he had not been wearing his seat belt.

Was it just a little inward intuition that caused him to put
on his seat belt? Was it the time he spent the night before,
consecrating his life and ministry to the Lord? Or was it one

of the members of our church climbing out of bed at four o'clock on the morning of the accident, kneeling by the bed and weeping tears of intercession in the Holy Ghost, praying for our staff? I do not know for sure what happened or exactly why it happened. But I do know our music minister was preserved through the power of God!

When Jesus told Simon Peter, "Satan hath requisitioned and received permission to have you," it could not have been good news to Peter.

How would you like to receive that prophetic message from God today? "Satan asked from God if he could have you, and He said, 'Take him; take your best shot.'"

God trusted Simon Peter because He knew his character. Today, as you mature in your faith, God trusts you because you are striving to be one in holiness with Him. He knows your character, and He has known your character from the beginning of time.

God said something to the devil that I pray every person will one day hear from the lips of our Heavenly Father:

> And the Lord said unto Satan, Hast thou considered my servant Job, that there is none like him in the earth, a perfect and an upright man, one that feareth God, and escheweth evil? and still he holdeth fast his integrity, although thou movedst me against him, to destroy him without cause. And Satan answered the Lord, and said, Skin for skin, yea, all that a man hath will he give for his life. But put forth thine hand now, and touch his bone and his flesh, and he will curse thee to thy face.
>
> —Job 2:3-5

God replied, "Not so, I know the man; I know him."

In the midst of the trials of life, it is one thing to know

God, but it is another thing to have God say, "I know this man. I know his heart, and I know he will faithfully serve me."

I want to be someone about which God can say those things. Don't you?

> When you are born again, filled with the Holy
> Ghost and start talking in tongues, the world might
> not want to rub shoulders with you anymore.
> —Pastor Rod Parsley

Job trusted God and stayed holy and faithful in the midst of trial. When trials hit your life, God wants you to trust Him and maintain a deep relationship so that you can experience His power and blessing.

What if the devil took away your home? Your job? Your kids? Your reputation?

What if the devil took all that away from you and you never get it back? After all, once a lie is told, it is told—it is impossible to untell it.

If you are faithful to the Gospel of Jesus Christ, the day will come when you will be the one under severe attack for serving Him. The world is going to make fun of you, so be prepared.

Early in 2004, the actor and director Mel Gibson released a movie, "The Passion of the Christ," which recounted the final hours of Jesus's life on earth. Even before the movie opened, news reports circulated that some Hollywood studio leaders had decided that no matter how much money the movie made, they would never work with Gibson again, because of his public pronouncements of faith surrounding the movie.

Now mind you, this is not a third-rate talent we're talking about. This is an actor whom fans have consistently paid good money to see in films, and an award-winning director. Over the course of his career, Gibson has been money in the bank for Hollywood studio executives. For them to declare their intention not to work with him is just one example that the Gospel—and those who claim it for their lives—is offensive to the unbeliever.

The world is going to laugh at you as well. You might even lose your job for your faith. Many people have had just that kind of trial in their lives, especially when the economy goes down. When it's time to lay people off, it's often easy to lay off the faithful Christians. So you may have to make a decision between your job and your faith.

It looked like Job had lost everything. It looked like he had every reason to turn his back on God.

But Job trusted God, and the Bible says,

> So the Lord blessed the latter end of Job more than his beginning: for he had fourteen thousand sheep, and six thousand camels, and a thousand yoke of oxen, and a thousand she asses.
>
> —Job 42:12

Although we may suffer persecution in the natural—in our bodies, our finances, our families—God will always redeem what was lost when we are faithful to His commands and obey His laws. Just like Job, God will bless you as you stay faithful!

'The best evidence of God's presence is the Devil's growl.' So said C.H. Spurgeon, and that little sentence has helped many a tried and tired child of God to stand fast and even to rejoice under the fiercest attacks of the foe. We read in the Book of Samuel that the moment David was crowned at Hebron, 'all the Philistines came up to seek David.' And the moment we get anything from the Lord worth contending for, the Devil comes to seek us.

—A. B. Simpson, Alliance Weekly

Take one fine boy of tender years,
Remove the ties of love,
Mix with parental neglect
and bad company in equal parts,
Sift in a few foul stories,
Add a dash of deviltry,
and a measure of mischief,
All to soak in,
then beat into a fury;
Add a pinch of hate,
then crush with brute force,
putting in a pound of parental cussing;
Shake well,
then turn into the street to harden;
Garnish with ungodliness
Serve with six months in the workhouse.

—Dr. C. H. Williamson

The thief cometh not, but for to steal, and to kill, and to destroy: I am come that they might have life, and that they might have it more abundantly.

—John 10:10

KEY 9:
KNOW THE DEVIL'S STRATEGIES

Put on the whole armour of God, that ye may be able to stand against the wiles of the devil.

—Ephesians 6:11

Satan is not original. What he has done to others, he will try to do to you. Satan operates within a very tight job description.

—Pastor Rod Parsley

Professional sports teams hire scouts; employees who go to games of opposing teams in order to determine the opponents' strengths and weaknesses. The scouts are paid to find out all they can about their opponents and report to the head coach. A head coach knows that information about an opponent's strategies is useful in planning to counteract those strategies. In many cases, effective scouting makes the difference between victory and defeat.

The same is true in the spirit realm. When you know the strategies of Satan, he cannot take you by surprise. When you know there is a spiritual war going on, you will not be vulnerable to the attack of the enemy. Knowing the devil's strategies can make the difference in your victory over sin and temptation.

He's a Liar

Adam and Eve were attacked by the devil in the form of a snake; they were deceived by a lie. Satan attacked the family structure of the first family, and as a result, curses fell on Adam and his children:

> Unto the woman he said, I will greatly multiply thy sorrow and thy conception; in sorrow thou shalt bring forth children; and thy desire shall be to thy husband, and he shall rule over thee. And unto Adam he said, Because thou hast hearkened unto the voice of thy wife, and hast eaten of the tree, of which I commanded thee, saying, Thou shalt not eat of it: cursed is the ground for thy sake; in sorrow shalt thou eat of it all the days of thy life; Thorns also and thistles shall it bring forth to thee; and thou shalt eat the herb of the field; In the sweat of thy face shalt thou eat bread, till thou return unto the ground; for out of it wast thou taken: for dust thou art, and unto dust shalt thou return.
>
> —Genesis 3:16-19

Look at the basic formula the devil used. It has not changed since man began walking on the face of the earth!

The devil's formula for destruction is: Lies + Sin = Family Destruction.

Lies: Satan lies to entice you to ignore God's will.

Sin: A sin is committed.

Family Destruction: Destruction and curses follow.

This same formula for destruction has been repeated countless times in history. For example:

Cain accepted the lie that his life would be better without Abel (lie).

Cain killed Abel (sin).

Cain was damaged and cursed. His family was destroyed (family destruction).

Throughout history, the names of the people have changed, but the strategy of the enemy, the formula he uses for destruction, has remained the same. The devil will use lies and deception to destroy you! Remember: Lies + Sin = Family Destruction.

Satan lies to the world and makes enticing promises he cannot deliver.

He promises the pregnant teenager tranquility and happiness—a less complicated life if she will just kill the fetus inside her womb.

He promises struggling marriage partners a new and trouble-free life with a new spouse if they will just end their current stress-ridden marriage through divorce.

He promises confused and frustrated parents they will somehow find relief from their feelings if they just beat and batter their hard-to-control child who is making too much noise.

Satan used a lie to remove Adam and Eve from the Garden of Eden, and his strategy has not changed.

In the early church, he was still at it, telling Ananias and Sapphira they could lie to the apostles about the value of land they had sold for the church's benefit. That lie cost Ananias his life:

> But Peter said, Ananias, why hath Satan filled thine heart to lie to the Holy Ghost, and to keep back part of the price of the land? Whiles it remained, was it not thine own? and after it was sold, was it not in thine own power? why hast thou conceived this thing in thine heart? thou hast not lied unto men, but unto God. And Ananias hearing these words fell

down, and gave up the ghost: and great fear came on all them that heard these things.

—Acts 5:3-5

Today, the devil's strategy is still the same. He will lie to you at every turn, trying to convince you there is something better outside the covenant of God:

• "If you will just have this one adulterous affair with that gorgeous woman, you will be happy."
• "If you do not tithe this month, your bills will be balanced and you can give double next month."
• "You don't need to fellowship with your church today. You can be a Christian without them."

The devil's strategy has not changed!

The best evidence I have that I am healed is because Satan tries to tell me, "You must die—you cannot live."

The best evidence I have that I am accepted by Jesus and the body of Christ is that the devil says, "You do not deserve to be called God's child."

The best evidence I have that I am walking in all of the abundant blessings of God is that the devil declares, "You are cursed. Every bad thing possible happens to you. Life could not get any worse."

A wise saint once said, "The only way you can tell if Satan is lying is if his lips move." Lying is the number one strategy of the enemy.

There are many today who are still listening to Satan's lies. He tells them "sickness and family problems are from God to teach you a lesson," and they listen.

He tells them, "If you are not healed, it is your fault because you do not have enough faith," and they listen.

He tells them, "You are not good enough to be in God's

family," and they listen.

You and I must refuse to listen to anything Satan says! Like water running off a duck's back, you must not entertain what he is saying for even one second. We must cast those lies out in the name of Jesus.

He's a Thief, Too!

The second strategy you can expect Satan to employ to attack you as a child of God is to try and steal anything he can from you.

If anything has been stolen in your life, Satan is the culprit.

The word translated "thief" in the King James version of the Bible is the Greek word "kleptes." We get the word "kleptomaniac" from this Greek word. The meaning of this word is "a thief by nature" or "a compulsive thief."

The devil is a calculating, deceptive plunderer. He moves freely in and out of unsuspecting lives. Every individual living in America has in some way been defrauded or robbed by this indiscriminate thief.

One good thing about identifying Satan as the thief is that God's Word tells us if the thief be caught he must restore what he has taken sevenfold! Solomon wrote:

> But if he be found, he shall restore sevenfold; he shall give all the substance of his house.
> —Proverbs 6:31

God is calling for us to bankrupt the kingdom of hell. We must demand that Satan return everything he has taken from us and return it sevenfold!

God has established a law of retribution for you! God has given you power over this thief! Jesus said,

Behold, I give unto you power to tread on serpents and scorpions, and over all the power of the enemy: and nothing shall by any means hurt you.
—Luke 10:19

The Killer of Joy

The third strategy Satan continues to employ against the saints is murder! The devil will attempt to kill your friends, your family, your joy, and your soul.

Satan is the mass murderer of the centuries. From the first animals slain to cover the nakedness of sin to the last of the remnant of Gog and Magog to die in the Apocalypse, Satan is the source of death!

With the inception of sin, death came into being, for the law of God states, "the wages of sin is death" (Romans 6:23).

But death need not come for the saints. Christ came to give us power over death. The author of Hebrews wrote,

Forasmuch then as the children are partakers of flesh and blood, he also himself likewise took part of the same; that through death he might destroy him that had the power of death, that is, the devil.
—Hebrews 2:14

Jesus defeated the grave. It has no victory. He prayed in the garden, "Father, if it be thy will, let this cup pass from me"; and in the Garden of Gethsemane, He prayed until his sweat became as great drops of blood. He said, "Nevertheless, not what I will, but what thou will, Father." And "for the joy that was set before him endured the cross, despising the shame, and is set down at the right hand of the throne of God" (Hebrews 12:2b).

God wants His people full of joy—the kind the devil can't steal, that discouragement can't dampen. There's no joy in hell, but in heaven there's joy unspeakable and full of glory.

The Bible says,

> Then he said unto them, Go your way, eat the fat, and drink the sweet, and send portions unto them for whom nothing is prepared: for this day is holy unto our Lord: neither be ye sorry; for the joy of the Lord is your strength.
>
> —Nehemiah 8:10

What's standing in the way of your joy? Pain? Infirmity? A rebellious spirit? A lying tongue? Perhaps you have allowed the devil to walk into your life, steal your joy, steal your anointing and steal your victory. If you let him, Satan will steal the glory of God right out of your life.

The Corruptive Touch

The final strategy of Satan is to destroy.

He soils and ruins everything he sees or touches. Contact with the devil means corruption and contamination.

No sinful pleasure can last; it is always just for a season. The end result of all sin must always be destruction. The apostle Paul wrote,

> For many walk, of whom I have told you often, and now tell you even weeping, that they are the enemies of the cross of Christ: Whose end is destruction, whose God is their belly, and whose

glory is in their shame, who mind earthly things.
—Philippians 3:18,19

God has a different end in mind for His children. As you recognize the strategies of Satan, and come against them for yourself and your family, you will win every victory. Paul reminds us of this unfailing promise,

Now thanks be unto God, which always causeth us to triumph in Christ, and maketh manifest the savour of his knowledge by us in every place.
—2 Corinthians 2:14

We have in the church of which I am a member, a woman who is very old, very deaf, and whose eyes are bad, but she is always at church, even though she does not hear a word. On Saturday she is given a church bulletin and she looks up and reads the hymns and Scripture lesson. One day she remarked that all she gets out of the service is that received from the bulletin, and I told her what a fine thing it is that she comes. She replied, "Well, you know, the Psalmist said, 'The Lord is in his holy temple, and I come here to meet the Lord.' Of how many who attend church can that be said, I wonder.

—Sunday School Times

Not forsaking the assembling of ourselves together, as the manner of some is; but exhorting one another: and so much the more, as ye see the day approaching.

—Hebrews 10:25

We are in a battlefield, not a recreation room.

—Pastor Rod Parsley

KEY 10:
RECEIVE LOCAL CHURCH POWER

Hebrews 10:25 tells us that the power of the corporate anointing makes corporate worship indispensable. One thing that is important to note about this Scripture is that it was written from a first-century perspective. These were people who worshiped together almost daily. From that perspective, we are admonished to worship God even more as we see "the day" approaching.

Tommy Hicks, a great man of God, had a vision of the church in the last days. He saw the church as a sleeping giant, bound by the shackles of religious tradition. He saw that the church would begin to wake up and shake off the bondages of the devil.

I do not think the church is awake yet. We are not yet serious about spiritual survival.

Many Christians just want to frolic in the flatlands of shallow spiritual experience. They go to church when they feel like it, pay their tithes when they feel like it, read their Bibles only occasionally and only know what someone else tells them about the Word of God.

They come to church and let someone spoon-feed them a little bit of spiritual pabulum. Then they go on their merry, fleshly, self-appeasing, self-satisfying, self-indulgent way, forgetting about everything they have been taught!

After all, they believe, God will make an exception for them.

The church is not a social club or a place to show off new clothes and flaunt self-indulgent lifestyles. We are in absolute, mortal conflict; and whether we realize it or not, we have an adversary who will destroy us unless we stand united through the church.

Remember, we are not alone. Our fellow Christians are in the same trenches with us. Each of us must help our brothers and sisters stay on guard. I am bone of your bone, flesh of your flesh. We must help each other guard against the enemy if we are going to face him.

When a brother falls, do not step on his head! Reach down and pick him up! He is your brother—ask him if there is anything you can do to help.

How much time have you spent in prayer lifting up the arms of others? How much time have you spent speaking life into them, asking God to guard their hearts? We must stop demanding so much more of everyone else than we do of ourselves. We must spiritually stand with one another. We must look at those around us and say, "I bless you and ask for God's protection upon your life, in Jesus' name."

You may ask, "What if they are in sin?"

Sin is God's business, not yours. But if you sense there is difficulty, then you can pray that God will reveal to them the horror of their sin and restore them into communion with Him.

Let us bless and strengthen each other.

Let us stand firmly in the trenches and support each other.

Let us get serious about survival.

Let us guard our hearts, and start to actively love our brothers and sisters in Christ through prayer.

You have the opportunity to be involved in

God's greatest instrument of revival, blessing, healing, salvation, and deliverance of our generation—
the local church.

—Pastor Rod Parsley

The Lord Jesus, our Redeemer, said,

> And I say also unto thee, That thou art Peter, and upon this rock I will build my church; and the gates of hell shall not prevail against it.
>
> —Matthew 16:18

Jesus did not say the gates of hell would not prevail against an evangelistic association or a teaching ministry. He did not say the gates of hell would not prevail against apostolic authority or the prophetic ministry. He said the gates of hell would not prevail against the church!

You say, "Well, He's talking about the universal church." We have a universal God; everything He does is universal in scope. God does have a church which is universal, intangible, and invisible; but that is not what I am referring to. I am referring specifically to the local church body God has prepared to give you the power to survive in your daily life.

Some say, "Well I'm saved, so that is all I need. I'm part of the universal church, so I don't have to belong to any local body or fellowship. Don't put that kind of bondage on me. I just go to church wherever I am led." On Sunday morning these folks stick their spiritual radar up to see where they're led. And for the vast majority of them, the only "led" they have is in the bottom of their seats. They're here, they're there, they're everywhere. These people are spiritual parasites. They just want to wallow around in the flat lands of shallow spiritual experience, picking up a scrap from the floor here and there that has fallen from the abundant table

God sets for His committed people! Spiritual parasites don't want commitment; they just want to float along.

When God wants us to see something universal or intangible, He always gives us a tangible representation of that intangible truth. The local church is a tangible representation of the universal church. It is the bricks-and-mortar representation of God's worldwide family.

When God wanted us to understand the relationship between our Redeemer and His church, He gave us the marriage covenant. When we look at a man and his wife, we see the relationship between Christ and His church.

Marriage is a covenant, a natural symbol of the universal spiritual union between Christ and His church that is unalterable. That is why marriage ceremonies often say "what God joins together, let no man put asunder." This is the same union He wants between His Son and His church.

Jesus died for every person of every race, every kindred, every tribe, every tongue who has ever walked on this planet or will ever walk on this planet. We are all baptized into one body—the universal church. You cannot touch it, you cannot see it, you cannot feel it. It is intangible and it is invisible, but that makes it no less real. If you are born again, you are part of the church of Jesus Christ.

When Jesus returns, He will gather His church unto Himself. We will be joined together with the saints from all the ages of time who have ever been or who ever will be after us. In that hour, we will see the universal church. But right now, we cannot see it.

So God gives us a natural, physical representation of that which we cannot see. He calls it the local body. You cannot function in that body without making a commitment.

After Christians came through the charismatic revival, many did not want to commit to a relationship in a local church. The only commitment most people wanted to make to a local church was, "I will stay there as long as they bless me. The very moment they do anything I don't like, I am out the door."

Hopefully, you did not make that kind of commitment to your spouse. Can you imagine? The first time someone burned the toast or forgot to fill the car up with gas, the marriage would be up in smoke!

God is looking for Christians willing to commit to their local church. Your pastor covenants to preach the gospel, to pray for you, to believe God for your miracles. In return, you covenant to commit to the church, to stick by your pastor, and to work together to reach lost souls in your community, in whatever your calling might be.

It is high time that the people sitting in the pews and the choir and the orchestra and the ushers and the greeters and the nursery workers and the children's ministry workers and the outreach workers and the volunteers who sweep the carpet and the people who work in the offices become as radically faithful to their calling as the people who stand behind the pulpit.

How Does God Want You 'Set'?

In Paul's discussion of spiritual gifts in 1 Corinthians 12, he writes that God "set," or placed, individuals in the church for specific necessary functions.

When you first pour concrete into a wooden form, it is called "green." If you remove the form from green concrete too soon, it just oozes, without form, all over the ground. And it's not very useful in that state. But there comes a time when concrete "sets," and the forms can be taken off, leaving the concrete slab to hold the integrity of its own shape.

Something similar happens in the Church. As you

mature in the Lord, the 'forms' can be taken away and your foundation can be established. When you are firmly 'set,' someone can come along and kick you, but you won't move. All that will happen is the person doing the kicking will stub their toe!

Not everyone is gifted to be an apostle, a prophet, an evangelist, a pastor, or a teacher. Not everyone has the gift of working of miracles or of healing. But there is one ministry that everyone has—the ministry of service. And in your local church body, it is vital that you serve wherever possible.

Rev. W. B. Godbey defined it this way: "Oh! The infinite value of the humble gospel helpers. Thousands of people who have no gifts as leaders but who are number one helpers. How grand revival work moves along when red hot platoons of fire-baptized helpers crowd around God's heroic leaders of the embattled hosts!"

The Church is engaged in spiritual warfare, and we need every single, solitary person ready and able to defend their battle station. Are you ready to confront the enemy with the 'weapons' God has provide for you?

Maybe your gifting is prayer.

Maybe your gifting is giving.

Maybe your gifting is ushering.

Maybe your gifting is taking care of the babies in the nursery and ministering to the next generation of saints.

No matter what your gifting is, you have a vital role to play in the local church—the neighborhood extension of the universal church. And your role in the spiritual battle we are fighting against the devil is a vital one. Some roles are more prominent than others, but no role is more important than any other.

It is time we start coming into the church doors with a "let me bless you" attitude instead of a "bless me" attitude. Let us ask our brothers and sisters, "How can I help you?

What can I do for you? Lord, I'm here to serve you. Show me my place, and I'll get in it. I'll go to work, and I'll be faithful."

It's time for us to get faithful. It is time to wake up and shake ourselves, and to commit to our local church.

We need to wake up, stir ourselves, and realize this is a spiritual conflict. If we are to be warriors in God's kingdom, we need to be spiritually prepared by contributing to the ministry of the church!

> How dare you run around thinking everything's supposed to pop up posies because you were in praise and worship for fifteen minutes? All you've done is jerked on the devil's chain!
>
> —Pastor Rod Parsley

We are invading enemy-held territory with the arsenal of God at our disposal. Yet, while some are brandishing swords and spears, others are waving around butter knives. Instead of carrying spiritual machine guns, many Christians are going into battle with squirt guns. And what's most demoralizing about this state of affairs is that the squirt-gun brigade is armed that way by choice.

The anointing of God, the gifting to be effective foes of the adversary, does not come free. You do not get it by watching television or by going about your business in the workplace. You receive the anointing in the presence of God, on your face with the Word open!

You may say, "Well, I wish I had the anointing." And I say: "No, you don't." Many Christians claim to want the anointing, but are only willing to invest the two hours you spend at church on Sunday morning for it. They want the victory without going into battle. It is time to depart from a nursery-school mentality and realize we are in the middle of a vicious spiritual war! This is spiritual life and death. It is not playing around; it is not take it or leave it.

Your individual life and the lives of our brothers and sisters depend on our commitment to fight spiritual warfare.

There was once an old codfish dealer, a very

earnest and sincere man, who lived prayerfully every day. One of the great joys of his life was the family worship hour. One year, two other merchants persuaded him to go into a deal with them by which they could control all the codfish in the market and greatly increase the price. The plan was succeeding well, when this good man learned that many poor people in Boston were suffering because of the great advance in the price of codfish. It troubled him so that he broke down in trying to pray at the family altar, and he went straight to the men who had led him into the plot and told them that he could not go on with it.

Said the old man: 'I cannot afford to do anything which interferes with my family prayers. And this morning when I got down on my knees and tried to pray, there was a mountain of codfish before me high enough to shut out the throne of God, and I could not pray. I tried my best to get around it or over it, but every time I started to pray that codfish loomed up between me and my God. I will not have my family prayers spoiled for all the codfish in the Atlantic Ocean. And I shall have nothing to do with this market control business, or with any money made from it.'

—Pentecostal Evangel

Children, obey your parents in the Lord: for this is right. Honour thy father and mother; (which is the first commandment with promise;) That it may be well with thee, and thou mayest live long on the earth.

—Ephesians 6:1-3

KEY 11:
DILIGENTLY GUARD YOUR FAMILY

Wives, submit yourselves unto your own husbands, as unto the Lord. For the husband is the head of the wife, even as Christ is the head of the church: and he is the saviour of the body. Therefore as the church is subject unto Christ, so let the wives be to their own husbands in every thing. Husbands, love your wives, even as Christ also loved the church, and gave himself for it; That he might sanctify and cleanse it with the washing of water by the word, That he might present it to himself a glorious church, not having spot, or wrinkle, or any such thing; but that it should be holy and without blemish. So ought men to love their wives as their own bodies. He that loveth his wife loveth himself. For no man ever yet hated his own flesh; but nourisheth and cherisheth it, even as the Lord the church.

—Ephesians 5:22-29

A gentle nudging of the Holy Ghost to pray, a split second of time, might make the difference between life and death.

—Pastor Rod Parsley

The greatest asset today's family has is the leading of the

Holy Ghost. We must learn to discern the prophetic voice of God. It is time to open our spiritual ears to the gentle wooing of the Holy Ghost, to learn to obey, to wake up and get serious.

We must learn to hear the quiet voice of God. It may be His gentle whisper saying, "No, do not go to the store right now; just worship Me a little while." And while you are worshiping Him, the devil's plan to meet you head-on with a truck is thwarted because you heard—and obeyed.

This is a survival strategy for the last days. There is an adversary who wants your family dead. He wants you out of the way; he wants you silenced. He will do anything he can do to stop you, because you are shaking his kingdom. Satan hates a godly family because he knows its spiritual strength. If Satan has his way, you will be walking around divorced or spinning into bankruptcy by this time next year.

The devil is causing families to become so caught up with obtaining worldly possessions they no longer have time to pray, read the Word, or worship together as a family. Evil forces are attacking families' finances, or the parents' attitudes toward finances, so that the parents work long hours, leaving little time for parents to spend with their children or with each other. Communication lines are being cut off. Many times they become so exhausted they are too tired to pray or to go to church.

Dads, if you have not prayed with your family in the last fifteen years, start today. Bless the food at the next meal, and then teach your children how to bless the food at future meals.

How much different family life would be if before any person in the household left home for the day everyone would join together in the living room, hold hands, unite together, and pray a hedge of protection around the entire family unit!

This is no time for us to sit back whining and complaining about what Satan is doing to attack and destroy our families and loved ones. It is time to fight!

This is no time for us to sit back in fear, waiting to see how Satan is going to attack our family next. It is time for Christian families to take the power and authority God has given to us and use it against the enemy!

When the children of Israel were preparing to enter their promised land, they were commanded not only to obey all the commandments of the covenant, but also commanded to remember all the great and mighty miracles God had done for them and to teach them to their children.

Moses said,

> Only take heed to thyself, and keep thy soul diligently, lest thou forget the things which thine eyes have seen, and lest they depart from thy heart all the days of thy life: but teach them thy sons, and thy sons' sons; Specially the day that thou stoodest before the Lord thy God in Horeb, when the Lord said unto me, Gather me the people together, and I will make them hear my words, that they may learn to fear me all the days that they shall live upon the earth, and that they may teach their children.
> —Deuteronomy 4:9,10

It is time for us to get our houses in order and teach our children about the mighty miracles of our loving God, who covers us with His protection. The spiritual strength of the church today depends upon the spiritual strength of its families.

Satan's strategy since Adam and Eve has been to tear down and destroy the spiritual foundation in the home. We must teach our children how to recognize and thwart the actions of the enemy.

Proverbs 22:6 tells us, "Train up a child in the way he should go: and when he is old, he will not depart from it." But in many homes, the Word of God has been replaced by television. The Bible is never even opened or read together as a family. It has been cast aside, neglected and almost forgotten.

It is time to reestablish the home as the spiritual foundation God intended it to be. Parents and grandparents must rise up in the spirit and make a new commitment to God that says, "As for me and my house, we will serve the Lord" (Joshua 24:15).

Men, it is time for you to take the position God has given you as head of your household. Accept your responsibility. Cover your family in prayer. Teach and train your children about God and His Word. It is not the responsibility of the church to teach your children about God—it is primarily your job. The local church is there to supplement the teaching and training your children receive at home. Work as a team with your wife to teach and nurture your children.

Women, if you are a single parent, or if your husband is unsaved or unwilling to accept his responsibility for the spiritual condition of your family, accept this as your responsibility. Establish your home as a spiritual training ground for your children. God will honor you and will anoint and strengthen you and your children.

Parents, determine now, regardless of the cost, no matter what battles you might face, that you and your family will serve and obey God.

A Christian convert from Hinduism was once asked if, for a certain salary, he was willing to go and try to commence a mission in a neighboring district where he would be sure to meet with great difficulties, and perhaps be persecuted and put to death. "I cannot do it for money," he replied, "but I can do it for Christ," and he went.

—Glad Tidings

And God hath set some in the church, first apostles, secondarily prophets, thirdly teachers, after that miracles, then gifts of healings, helps, governments, diversities of tongues.

—1 Corinthians 12:28

If you are called and equipped as a farmer, leave lion taming alone. The reason for such falling away in the ranks of God is that too many people are operating outside their calling.

—Pastor Rod Parsley

KEY 12:
GET SET IN THE CHURCH

Another key for God's protection in these perilous times is to find your place and get set. The apostle Paul wrote, "For the gifts and calling of God are without repentance" (Romans 11:29).

What has God called you to do? The anointing follows the calling.

If you are not anointed to do a given work, stay away from it. Otherwise, you will find yourself working in the flesh, and your ability will be limited to your own strength. In your own ability and strength, the devil will defeat you every single time.

To be the best servant of God you can be, find the place God has anointed you to serve, the place where you can be most effective in the local church and fill it. No task God has called you to do is demeaning. Not everyone is called to preach or to prophesy. The ministry of helps is a vital function in the body of Christ. For example, many are called to be armourbearers. The function of an armourbearer in Bible times was to hold the shield and carry the sword of a warrior. Even King David started out that way:

And David came to Saul, and stood before him: and he loved him greatly; and he became his armourbearer.

—1 Samuel 16:21

Ephesians six stresses the importance of our armor. Verse sixteen states, "Above all, taking the shield of faith, wherewith ye shall be able to quench all the fiery darts of the wicked." Everyone is responsible for their own personal faith, but that corporate shield of faith is held up by armourbearers. If they do not show up, no matter how strong the leader's personal faith may be, the leader will be unprotected, and the ministry will be subject to the fiery darts of the enemy.

No matter what place in the local body God has placed you, He has called each of us to intercede, to travail, to mourn and to be armourbearers for His church. He needs us to stand in the gap for lost souls in our communities, nation and world. In the Bible God says,

And I sought for a man among them, that should make up the hedge, and stand in the gap before me for the land, that I should not destroy it: but I found none. Therefore have I poured out mine indignation upon them; I have consumed them with the fire of my wrath: their own way have I recompensed upon their heads, saith the Lord God.

—Ezekiel 22:30,31

The Day of the Lord is drawing near. Judgment, such as the world has never known, is coming upon this earth—and God is looking for spiritual warriors who will stand in the gap for individuals, and for His church.

Just as Jesus made intercession for the world through His life and death, and has reconciled us to God, we have been given the ministry of reconciliation for the church:

And all things are of God, who hath reconciled

120

us to himself by Jesus Christ, and hath given to us the ministry of reconciliation; To wit, that God was in Christ, reconciling the world unto himself, not imputing their trespasses unto them; and hath committed unto us the word of reconciliation. Now then we are ambassadors for Christ, as though God did beseech you by us: we pray you in Christ's stead, be ye reconciled to God.

—2 Corinthians 5:18-20

Be a need-meeter in your local body of believers. Allow God to flow through your life in prayer and through your actions. Cry out to God on behalf of the lost around you. Enter into the bowels of intercession for the sin and corruption around you. Cry out to God for His mercy.

When the trials of your faith come, and you feel like bowing down under their weight, remember the three Hebrew children and the fiery furnace. They did not bow, and they did not burn.

—Pastor Rod Parsley

Shadrach, Meshach, and Abednego declared, in the face of certain destruction, that they would continue to serve their God. While everyone around them bowed to King Nebuchadnezzar and worshiped him, they stood straight and worshiped God alone. They were set in the ways of their God.

The book of Daniel records what happened as a result of their stand for God. They were thrown into a furnace so hot that the guards who placed them there were consumed by the flames. But the Hebrews weren't even touched by the scent of smoke! (See Daniel 3:27.)

Learn to look beyond the fiery furnace. It is time we

allowed God to take us through the furnace, through the trial, and through the tribulation. When He brings us out on the other side and we will not even smell like smoke, we will proclaim for all to hear: "There is a God in Israel who is able to deliver."

Place your confidence and trust in the delivering power of God to bring you through. And when you are going through, remember, like Shadrach, Meshach and Abednego, you are just going through!

As you and I become stronger we can pray for others. Our prayers will make the body of Christ a unified, strong body of believers who are determined not just to resist the enemy, but to absolutely destroy him!

The Day of the Lord is coming—when Christ will return and judgment will come upon the earth.

As we become set in the church and accept our spiritual responsibilities, God will empower us to turn entire nations around for His glory. It is God's plan and purpose to use us to save untold thousands from the destruction that is coming. Can you hear it?

By His Spirit, God is sounding an alarm. He is looking for men and women who, like Shadrach, Meshach and Abednego, will walk through the fiery furnace on behalf of lost souls.

I am more determined than ever to grasp hold of the hands of those who are in the foxhole with me. I need you, as members of the body of Christ—no matter who you are or where you are—to pray for me, just as I pray for you. Like Aaron and Hur, armourbearers must keep the hands of God's leaders uplifted. Only then can the victory of the corporate church be won.

I am determined to point my finger in the devil's face and command him to take his hands off you and off the church. I am determined that the blessings of God will be released in your life.

Every great movement of God can be traced to a kneeling figure! Therefore, 'Ye that make mention of the Lord, KEEP NOT SILENCE' (Isaiah 6:6).

—D. L. Moody

Praying always with all prayer and supplication in the Spirit, and watching thereunto with all perseverance and supplication for all saints.

—Ephesians 6:18

Prayer of intercession is urgent prayer in known or unknown tongues for divine intervention on behalf of a pressing need.

—Pastor Rod Parsley

KEY 13:
PRAY ALWAYS

There are seven types of prayer, and all seven need to be active in your life.

1) The Prayer of Agreement
Jesus said,

> Again I say unto you, That if two of you shall agree on earth as touching any thing that they shall ask, it shall be done for them of my Father which is in heaven.
>
> —Matthew 18:19

Having a prayer partner who can come into agreement with you in prayer greatly multiplies your effectiveness. The best possible agreement is between a godly husband and wife.

2) The Prayer of Faith
The Bible says, "And the prayer of faith shall save the sick, and the Lord shall raise him up; and if he have committed sins, they shall be forgiven him" (James 5:15).

The prayer of faith will move any mountain. To pray the prayer of faith, it is necessary for one first to have faith. Faith is built on God's Word and our relation to the Word and to God.

Dr. Lester Sumrall put it this way: "Faith is simply knowing God."

3) The Prayer of Consecration

The prayer of consecration sets something or someone apart to God's exclusive service. In 1 Samuel 1, we see where Hannah, consecrates—sets apart—her son Samuel to the service of God. In the New Testament, God consecratd His people to Himself when He said, "But ye are a chosen generation, a royal priesthood, an holy nation, a peculiar people; that ye should shew forth the praises of him who hath called you out of darkness into his marvellous light (1 Peter 2:9).

4) The Prayer of Thanksgiving

The prayer of thanksgiving gives praise for what God has done. The apostle Paul wrote, "Be careful for nothing; but in every thing by prayer and supplication with thanksgiving let your requests be made known unto God" (Philippians 4:6).

5) Prayer in the Spirit

Prayer in the Spirit is exactly that—prayer in a language that comes from the Spirit of God and not from our own understanding. In the Book of Jude we are told, "But ye, beloved, building up yourselves on your most holy faith, praying in the Holy Ghost" (vs. 20). The apostle Paul wrote,

> For he that speaketh in an unknown tongue speaketh not unto men, but unto God: for no man understandeth him; howbeit in the spirit he speaketh mysteries.
>
> —1 Corinthians 14:2

6) Prayer of Intercession
The prayer of intercession is urgent prayer in known or unknown tongues that intercedes on behalf of another.

> Likewise the Spirit also helpeth our infirmities: for we know not what we should pray for as we ought: but the Spirit itself maketh intercession for us with groanings which canot be uttered
> —Romans 8:26

As our intercessor, Jesus identified with man. He did not elevate Himself above us, but rather humbled Himself and was made in the likeness of men. In identifying with us, He was willing to lay down His divine attributes and become like us, sharing the same human nature and being made like us in all respects.

The author of Hebrews said of Jesus,

> Forasmuch then as the children are partakers of flesh and blood, he also himself likewise took part of the same; that through death he might destroy him that had the power of death, that is, the devil; And deliver them who through fear of death were all their lifetime subject to bondage. For verily he took not on him the nature of angels; but he took on him the seed of Abraham. Wherefore in all things it behoved him to be made like unto his brethren, that he might be a merciful and faithful high priest in things pertaining to God, to make reconciliation for the sins of the people.
> —Hebrews 2:14-17

7) Prayer of Authority
How do you pray the prayer of authority? You learn how to "bind and loose" in the name of Jesus. In Matthew 16:19,

Jesus said, "And I will give unto thee the keys of the kingdom of heaven: and whatsoever thou shalt bind on earth shall be bound in heaven: and whatsoever thou shalt loose on earth shall be loosed in heaven."

> In the heat of the conflict, you cannot afford to
> be out of touch with your Commander-in-Chief.
> —Pastor Rod Parsley

Prayer is our communication link with the Lord.

God wants you to stay within calling distance. If you are out of touch, you experience a break in the lines of communication from headquarters. When that happens, you become motivated and manipulated by your old nature.

When communication is cut off from God, your desires and actions stem from your deceived flesh; your ears become deaf to the sweet, soft voice of the living Creator. Wise up and wake up! You have an adversary and he will kill you if you will let him.

I believe with all my heart that if we will learn to recognize the inward witness of the Holy Ghost, we will be able to avoid many of the schemes of the devil. You will learn to recognize that voice through communication with God, through prayer.

When you begin to pray, you have access into the spirit realm. That's where God is. When you pray to God, He will begin to reveal to you the root causes of the battles you are facing.

Your battle is not against any sickness or any disease the enemy has put upon your body. Your battle is not with your spouse, your children or any other family member. Your battle is not with your boss or your fellow employees. Your battle is not with your financial condition. Your battle is in the spirit realm.

We must wake up and recognize that behind the circumstances we are facing, there are spiritual powers and rulers of darkness at work. Behind political struggles in our nation and around the world, there are evil forces at work. There are spirits of confusion, fear, frustration, promiscuity, homosexuality, lust, envy, jealousy, hatred, violence, rebellion, murder, suicide, resentment, selfishness, and many others at work. They are killing, stealing, and destroying.

Before we can tear down the strongholds the enemy has built in our home, city, and nation, we must first know the enemy—the spirit forces that are the root cause of our circumstances.

The only way we can have the sharp spiritual eyes necessary to know and recognize the enemy is through prayer! Without prayer, the Christian is like a blindfolded soldier without a weapon. He or she is unable to see the enemy, and without the firepower to destroy him.

Just as God anointed Jesus with the Holy Spirit and gave Him power and authority to destroy the works of the devil, He has given us power and authority over all the power of the enemy.

God has given us the authority to bind and loose. Jesus said, "Verily I say unto you, Whatsoever ye shall bind on earth shall be bound in heaven: and whatsoever ye shall loose on earth shall be loosed in heaven" (Matthew 18:18). The spiritual key to releasing that power and authority is prayer.

To survive these perilous times, the battle must first be won on your face before God. We must commit to fight against the forces of darkness with the mighty weapon of prayer.

God's covering is assured when we pray.

Only take heed to thyself, and keep thy soul diligently, lest thou forget the things which thine eyes have seen, and lest they depart from thy heart all the days of thy life: but teach them thy sons, and thy sons' sons.

—Deuteronomy 4:9

Let your heart therefore be perfect with the Lord our God, to walk in his statutes, and to keep his commandments, as at this day.

—1 Kings 8:61

And if thou wilt walk before me, as David thy father walked, in integrity of heart, and in uprightness, to do according to all that I have commanded thee, and wilt keep my statutes and my judgments.

—1 Kings 9:4

We must place a guard on our hearts and exercise extreme care over what we let in.

—Pastor Rod Parsley

KEY 14:
GUARD YOUR HEART

Your heart must have but one master—God Almighty. King Solomon wrote, "Keep thy heart with all diligence; for out of it are the issues of life" (Proverbs 4:23).

We must be careful what our eyes see and our ears hear and of the company we keep.

There is only one way for the devil to get a place in our hearts—we have to give it to him. There is a song that says:

"Satan, don't be deceived, you're not getting by
When His army intercedes—you're identified
Stand back you spirits of darkness
Stay out of this dwelling place
We will war against all evil with praise."

Ephesians 4:27 says, "Neither give place to the devil." The word "place" comes from the very interesting Greek word "topos." It means several things, including "a position of opportunity." So Paul is saying we should never give the devil a position of opportunity—such as sin—to enter our lives.

Jesus' admonishment for the church at Ephesus included these words: "Remember therefore from whence thou art fallen, and repent, and do the first works; or else I will come unto thee quickly, and will remove thy candlestick out of his place, except thou repent" (Revelation 2:5). Jesus is saying to the Ephesians, "If you do not repent, if you do not guard your heart against sin, I will come and remove your candle-stick out of its place. I will move your church out of its position of opportunity."

God gives every person and every church a position of opportunity. In Ephesians 4:27, God is also saying, "Do not give the devil any position of opportunity." Why? Because he will seize on that opportunity. The devil will bring you down into the eternal death of hell if you let him.

When we guard our hearts, we enter the realm of the spirit, and we deny the devil access into our spiritual affairs. You and I must not wait until the devil moves in and unpacks his suitcase of blight and discouragement to kick him out. It is much easier to head the devil off at the pass.

Guard your heart to survive.

Worship is "that which comes down from the Father, by the Son, in the power of the Spirit, through the human instrument and goes up by the power of the Holy Spirit, through the Son, to the Father.

—A. P. Gibbs

Hast thou not known? hast thou not heard, that the everlasting God, the Lord, the Creator of the ends of the earth, fainteth not, neither is weary? there is no searching of his understanding. He giveth power to the faint; and to them that have no might he increaseth strength. Even the youths shall faint and be weary, and the young men shall utterly fall: But they that wait upon the Lord shall renew their strength; they shall mount up with wings as eagles; they shall run, and not be weary; and they shall walk, and not faint.

—Isaiah 40:28-31

Complacency is a sickening cancer eating away at the power of the New Testament church.

—Pastor Rod Parsley

And it shall come to pass afterward, that I will pour out my spirit upon all flesh; and your sons and your daughters shall prophesy, your old men shall dream dreams, your young men shall see visions: And also upon the servants and upon the handmaids in those days will I pour out my spirit.

—Joel 2:28,29

KEY 15:
WORSHIP GOD!

Joel prophesied that revival was coming! Holiness, prayer, praise, and worship bring revival.

Peter stood up on the day of Pentecost and said the revival Joel had prophesied had begun.

> For these are not drunken, as ye suppose, seeing it is but the third hour of the day. But this is that which was spoken by the prophet Joel.
>
> —Acts 2:15,16

A great revival started this age, and it will end with an even greater revival. The revival that is coming on the earth will make every other revival the world has ever known look like a Sunday school picnic. An unprecedented outpouring of the glory of God is about to fall on this earth!

We are in the beginnings of the last great end-time revival, and the church needs to wake up and see what God is doing in the earth. Walls are falling down, and people are hearing the Gospel who have never heard it before.

Revival is moving across this land, and we will never be the same. When there is revival, saints get right with God. When there is revival, the power of God is in manifestation.

Praise and worship are two key spiritual ingredients to release revival.

Worship is part of our service to God, and keeps us in an attitude of reverence. Praise and worship draw us close to God, and help us to better know His will for our lives. Under the New Covenant, praise is our sacrifice, replacing the perfect lamb and other sacrifices of the Old Law. The author of Hebrews wrote,

> By him therefore let us offer the sacrifice of praise to God continually, that is, the fruit of our lips giving thanks to his name.
>
> —Hebrews 13:15

Under the old law, the people were told to bring the first fruits of their labors in the field to God. Under the new covenant, we are asked to bring the "fruit of our lips" as a sacrifice to our heavenly Father.

We are encouraged to praise God in everything we do. As the Psalmist wrote,

> Praise ye the Lord. Praise God in his sanctuary: praise him in the firmament of his power. Praise him for his mighty acts: praise him according to his excellent greatness. Praise him with the sound of the trumpet: praise him with the psaltery and harp. Praise him with the timbrel and dance: praise him with stringed instruments and organs. Praise him upon the loud cymbals: praise him upon the high sounding cymbals. Let every thing that hath breath praise the Lord. Praise ye the Lord.
>
> —Psalm 150

I believe there are people today who want life.

They are tired of the doldrums and drudgery of yesterday, and they want fresh oil.

—Pastor Rod Parsley

True worship is placing our entire lives—all we deem valuable—at the feet of Jesus. So much will be accomplished in our lives if we follow the pattern Mary employed:

Then took Mary a pound of ointment of spikenard, very costly, and anointed the feet of Jesus, and wiped his feet with her hair: and the house was filled with the odour of the ointment.

—John 12:3

If we submit to the lordship of Jesus as Mary did, then we will open new vistas of worship and power far greater than we ever dreamed.

I believe there are people today who want life. They are tired of the doldrums and drudgery of yesterday, and they want fresh oil. They want a new life, a new beginning, a new vision, and a new strength. They want a new ability, a new anointing, and a new fervency in God. When we achieve this, it will make the devil angry. He thinks he has the church lulled to sleep, but every time he has the church at this point, we prove him wrong.

My father used to pride himself on being able to keep a fire going. I have seen the character of my Heavenly Father many times in my natural father. Every night my Dad would bank our fire. When the time came to go to bed, he would scoop up all the day's ashes and pile them on top of the fire. I would say, "Dad, why are you doing that? Why don't you just let it burn out?"

He would say, "No, I am preserving it."

He would take those ashes and pack them down on top

of the fire; without oxygen, the fire would smolder into a heap of grayness.

Skeptics may think the church is just a lump of gray and lifeless matter from yesterday—that it is not burning and glowing. But I have news for them!

In the morning when my Dad climbed out of bed, he would start to fan away those ashes on top of the heap. He would begin to blow on the coals underneath, and ignited by the oxygen of his breath, the embers from yesterday's fire burst into flame!

The Bible says,

> And they that shall be of thee shall build the old waste places: thou shalt raise up the foundations of many generations; and thou shalt be called, The repairer of the breach, The restorer of paths to dwell in.
>
> —Isaiah 58:12

God is going to rekindle the fires of revival in the church of Jesus Christ, and this generation will go forth to repair the breach the devil has created between God and the people.

It is time for you and me to start talking to our unsaved friends and family members about the love of Jesus and the power of the Holy Ghost. We must lose sight of men and start proclaiming the majesty of Jesus. We must extol and magnify His name.

There are changes going on in the body of Christ. Paul said,

> While we look not at the things which are seen, but at the things which are not seen: for the things which are seen are temporal; but the things which are not seen are eternal.
>
> —2 Corinthians 4:18

In this verse, the word "temporal" means "subject to change." God is moving on the church.

There are men and women of God who are being raised up with the same stature as a Martin Luther, with the same fervency of a John Wesley, with the same power of one named John who came out of the wilderness eating locusts and wild honey, declaring, "Repent ye: for the kingdom of heaven is at hand" (Matthew 3:2).

God is raising up people with the fervency of Jesus. Some of them will be nationally prominent leaders. Others will be heroes only in their own households. But all of them will be focused on telling others that God has the solution for living in perilous times. I fully believe that we may be the generation chosen to usher in the coming of the Lord.

God is raising up some people who, like John the Baptist, are saying, "He must increase, but I must decrease" (John 3:30). Many men and women in the church today would just as soon preach behind a curtain as before the multiplied millions. God is raising up some powerful men—not only in the pulpit, but also in the pew.

God is raising up some families who are going to herald the coming of the Lord in the corridors of the local school, in the aisles of the neighborhood grocery store and on the playground of the neighborhood park. They are going to prophetically declare as John the Baptist did: "Behold the Lamb of God, which taketh away the sin of the world" (John 1:29b).

But incredibly, not everyone in the church is preparing for this exciting time. Complacency is a cancer eating away at the power of the New Testament church. Far too many people are content with their present life on this earth to long for the life to come. They say, "Let someone else do it. Let someone else pray. Let someone else witness. Let someone else storm the gates of hell. I will sit here in my padded pew and raise my hands once a week." I don't understand how people can get complacent in these perilous times, but they surely do.

We must lovingly rouse our brothers and sisters from their complacency, because we need them to battle along with us.

We have a heritage in the Lord, an inheritance of the saints. We have been given glowing coals from the altar of God and He has placed them on the inside of us. And now, He is breathing Holy Spirit oxygen upon us to fan a flame that will cause revival to spread to the four corners of the earth. Our generation has never seen the kind of revival that God will bring as this age draws to a close.

It is time to go forward, to do more than we have ever done before. It is time to pray without ceasing, to witness with a fervency only the Holy Ghost can give, to praise and worship our God with every fiber of our being so men and women will be convicted of their sins by the glory of the presence of Jesus Christ upon our lives. Praise and worship are our mighty weapons of war.

Nehemiah had never seen revival in his generation. He had only heard there used to be a flame in Jerusalem, and the hand of Yahweh delivered His people—His right arm brought them great victory. But Nehemiah did not know anything about it, just like this generation does not know anything about real revival.

We do not know what revival is like, nor do we sometimes appear to care what it would be like if a new and mighty revival, ushered in by the breath of God, would explode upon our dying world.

We do not understand. We have only heard about it, and some of us have not even cared to hear about it. We do not know what it is like to come two hours early to a service because sinners are pouring into the church, crying out and searching for God. We're more concerned with whether we will be able to find a parking space and whether or not one of the newcomers to our congregation will sit in 'our' usual pew!

Revival is coming. Will we be ready? We are either going to be set ablaze through praise and worship or stagnate in sin. It's our choice.

Miss C. Lefinwell, a missionary in China, gave the following account of deliverance from death by the Boxers: "There was a lady missionary whom the Boxers told to kneel down as they prepared to cut off her head. She knelt as told, but as she did so, she looked up into the man's face and actually smiled. As she looked at him a moment, thus smiling, it seemed as if his face began to change and to reflect the smile. He stepped back a little, and then continued to withdraw, together with his companions, until after a little they all fled, leaving the lady alone. As the Boxers were retreating the leader turned and said to her: 'You cannot die. You are immortal.' If her face had shown fear, they would have killed her without hesitation. I suppose the smile seemed supernatural. She afterward said, 'I did not know that I smiled.'"

—Life of a Missionary

Fear thou not; for I am with thee: be not dismayed; for I am thy God: I will strengthen thee; yea, I will help thee; yea, I will uphold thee with the right hand of my righteousness.

—Isaiah 41:10

The Bible said in the last days men's hearts will fail them for fear. But do not hang your head down or wring your hands, because He was not talking about you.

—Pastor Rod Parsley

KEY 16:
FEAR ONLY GOD

I do not have a spirit of fear, because fear is not of God. The apostle Paul wrote, "For God hath not given us the spirit of fear; but of power, and of love, and of a sound mind" (2 Timothy 1:7).

If you have a spirit of fear, you did not acquire it from God, because He said,

> Fear thou not; for I am with thee: be not dismayed; for I am thy God: I will strengthen thee; yea, I will help thee; yea, I will uphold thee with the right hand of my righteousness.
> —Isaiah 41:10

You may say, "But, Pastor Rod, you do not know what is going on at my house." And you're right, I don't. But you don't have to be dismayed about what is going on at your house. In fact, Jesus commanded us not to be dismayed:

> Let not your heart be troubled: ye believe in God, believe also in me. In my Father's house are many mansions: if it were not so, I would have told you. I go to prepare a place for you. And if I go and prepare a place for you, I will come again, and

receive you unto myself; that where I am, there ye may be also.

—John 14:1-3

So fear not.

The Bible said in the last days men's hearts will fail them for fear:

Men's hearts failing them for fear, and for look-ing after those things which are coming on the earth: for the powers of heaven shall be shaken.

—Luke 21:26

The end times will be like living a nightmare every day for those who have not been born again. Nations will col-lapse; economies will come apart at the seams; we will see turmoil, trouble, strife, hunger, famine, pestilence, earth-quakes, and rumors of wars. The Bible promises as much:

And ye shall hear of wars and rumours of wars: see that ye be not troubled: for all these things must come to pass, but the end is not yet. For nation shall rise against nation, and kingdom against kingdom: and there shall be famines, and pestilences, and earthquakes, in divers places. All these are the beginning of sorrows.

—Matthew 24:6-8

God said the last days will be horrific. Everyday life will be more frightening than a horror movie. It will take a bag of gold to buy a piece of bread. Epidemics like AIDS will sweep the continents.

Today, when someone gets a little mole on their face, the devil screams his lie: "Cancer! Your grandmother died of it, and now it is going to get you, too."

My grandfather was taking an aspirin one night, and my

father said, "Well, Dad, do you have a headache?"

"No," he replied, "I am taking this in case I get one."

Don't laugh; you do the same thing. You go to the drug store, and you need a grocery cart to carry out the over-the-counter medications and vitamins and supplements and low-carb diet items you buy. You are expecting to have health issues.

People are fearful for what may happen to them and their families. Nearly one marriage in two ends in divorce; children are growing up without parents; twelve-year-olds and thirteen-year-olds are having babies. Kids are shooting up dope. Sexually transmitted diseases are up seventy-five percent since 1960. Sexual promiscuity is rampant, leaving unplanned pregnancies and sexually transmitted diseases in its wake. It is scary out there!

The Bible said in the last days men's hearts will fail them for fear. The same Bible that said men's hearts would fail them for fear also says "fear not." Jesus said, "But even the very hairs of your head are all numbered. Fear not therefore: ye are of more value than many sparrows" (Luke 12:7).

Why should we be free from fear? Because Jesus promised us his presence. He said: "Lo, I am with you alway, even unto the end of the world. Amen" (Matthew 28:20b).

In Jeremiah, God said,

> Be not afraid of their faces: for I am with thee to deliver thee, saith the Lord. Then the Lord put forth his hand, and touched my mouth. And the Lord said unto me, Behold, I have put my words in thy mouth. See, I have this day set thee over the nations and over the kingdoms, to root out, and to pull down, and to destroy, and to throw down, to build, and to plant.
> —Jeremiah 1:8-10

As people of the Spirit, we do not need to be troubled or dismayed. In fact, we have every reason to be bold! God has given us the power to rule over kingdoms and to root out and destroy the enemy!

A definition for fear that uses the word as an acronym is False Evidence Appearing Real. By this definition, fear is an illusion. It is the counterfeit of faith. They are mutually exclusive and cancel one another out. Fear and faith cannot live in the same heart.

What happens tomorrow will not surprise or astound Jesus. He wrote the book. He said, "In the last days men will run to and fro like a bunch of ants on an anthill, running everywhere and nowhere."

When the time comes for Jesus to return, men's hearts will fail them because they are full of fear. They will fear for their children's lives, and for their own lives. Job said, "Behold, the fear of the Lord, that is wisdom; and to depart from evil is understanding" (Job 28:28).

The fear of the Lord is a healthy fear, since it is the beginning of wisdom. But we need not fear the empty lies of the devil.

One of the most-memorized passages in all of Scripture shows the peace we should have in the face of fear.

> The Lord is my shepherd; I shall not want. He maketh me to lie down in green pastures: he leadeth me beside the still waters. He restoreth my soul: he leadeth me in the paths of righteousness for his name's sake. Yea, though I walk through the valley of the shadow of death, I will fear no evil: for thou art with me; thy rod and thy staff they comfort me.
> —Psalm 23:1-4

Did you think that the Lord had a shepherd's rod because

He was so old He could hardly get around? No! He had it as a weapon against predators. My heavenly Father is my shepherd. His rod and His staff comfort and protect me.

Tomorrow will be no surprise to my God. You and I do not need to fear tomorrow, for the Lord of Glory has preceded us into the future and prepared a way for us.

Another psalm in the Bible models the confidence we should have in our God's protection of His children;

> There shall no evil befall thee, neither shall any plague come nigh thy dwelling. For he shall give his angels charge over thee, to keep thee in all thy ways. They shall bear thee up in their hands, lest thou dash thy foot against a stone. Thou shalt tread upon the lion and adder: the young lion and the dragon shalt thou trample under feet. Because he hath set his love upon me, therefore will I deliver him: I will set him on high, because he hath known my name. He shall call upon me, and I will answer him: I will be with him in trouble; I will deliver him, and honour him.
>
> —Psalm 91:10-15

With the world falling apart around us, we can know we are safe.

With AIDS, cancer, and other diseases devastating the world population, we can know we are safe.

With terrorists actively seeking opportunities for our demise because of who we are and what we believe, we can know we are safe.

With a tenuous economy threatening our material security, we can know we are safe—because we are covered by a God who is committed to protecting His children.

He walks with me. He talks with me, and nothing on the face of this earth shall harm me. Greater is my God who is in me, in front of me, behind me, beside me, beneath me, and above me than the devil that is the prince of this world.

The apostle John wrote, "Ye are of God, little children, and have overcome them: because greater is he that is in you, than he that is in the world" (1 John 4:4).

I am not afraid of tomorrow. If this hunk of clay falls over in the next thirty seconds, do not weep for me, because I will be seated in heavenly places. Carry on the vision and keep right on preaching. I will be cheering—for the last foe to be defeated in the arena of fear is the fear of death—and I am not afraid.

Why fear what the economy is going to do?

Why are you afraid of losing your job?

Why are you afraid things are falling apart around you?

Why are you afraid to walk down the street?

Why are you afraid to turn on the news?

We do not need to fear anything, because we have been saved by the blood of our Lord and Savior Jesus Christ.

You and I need to get a revelation of Jesus standing, battle-scarred, with His staff in one hand and the keys of the kingdom in the other. He has been in conflict, and He is victorious! So we do not need to be afraid of eternity, because He has already gone before us. Jesus is our way-maker.

You say, "Pastor Rod, my circumstances are so bad, I do not know if there is any way out."

Yes, there is! I know that Jesus is a way-maker, because He made a way for me. When my heart was dark and weary, Jesus came and answered my prayer. He brought me out of darkness and into light, out of death and into life, out of chains and into freedom.

He did it for me, and He will do it for you!

But call to remembrance the former days, in which, after ye were illuminated, ye endured a great fight of afflictions.

—Hebrews 10:32

Do you know what God is telling the body of Christ today? Take your dreams, your plans, your hopes, your aspirations, and the things you love the most and give them to me.

—Pastor Rod Parsley

KEY 17:
HOLD FAST TO HIS WORD

God will champion the cause of His elect. He will bare His right arm to them that bow the knee to Him.

I want God to do something in me—to take tribulation and turn it into triumph, so I can be a witness. I want to be able to show that He who lives in me is greater than he that is in the world. If we do not have something better than the world has, then we have nothing to preach about. I believe we do have something better than the world, and we should climb to the housetops and shout it out loud.

God spoke to Abraham and said,

Now the Lord had said unto Abram, Get thee out of thy country, and from thy kindred, and from thy father's house, unto a land that I will shew thee: And I will make of thee a great nation, and I will bless thee, and make thy name great; and thou shalt be a blessing: And I will bless them that bless thee, and curse him that curseth thee: and in thee shall all families of the earth be blessed.

—Genesis 12:1-3

But Abraham tried to take things into his own hands, and the result was Ishmael. God said, "He is not the one. You

151

tried it your way, now try it mine."

The Bible says Sarah conceived and brought forth a child, and they called him Isaac. Isaac grew up to be a young man much loved by his father. And every time his father saw him, he saw the promise of God and the fulfillment of his spiritual destiny. But do you know what God said to Abraham?

> And he said, Take now thy son, thine only son Isaac, whom thou lovest, and get thee into the land of Moriah; and offer him there for a burnt offering upon one of the mountains which I will tell thee of.
> —Genesis 22:2

On the mountain, Abraham lifted up his hand to slay his son, and God stopped it in midair. He said, "I have seen your heart."

> And he said, Lay not thine hand upon the lad, neither do thou any thing unto him: for now I know that thou fearest God, seeing thou hast not withheld thy son, thine only son from me.
> —Genesis 22:12

Today, God is asking us to give up much of what we hold dear. He is saying, "Take your dreams, your plans, your hopes, your aspirations—the things you love the most—and give them to Me."

There is so much about the Christian life that the unregenerate heart cannot understand:

• Only in death is there life—by dying to yourself and heeding the Word of God.

• The way to live is to die.

• The way to receive is to give.

• The way to win is to surrender.

Take your Bible and hold it in your hands. Open it up
and leaf through its pages. The Book you hold in your hand
is God's Word to you! It is sacred and holy. Every word in it,
from cover to cover, is divinely inspired. A solemn warning
is given to those who would add to or take away from the
words that are written in it:

> For I testify unto every man that heareth the
> words of the prophecy of this book, If any man shall
> add unto these things, God shall add unto him the
> plagues that are written in this book: And if any man
> shall take away from the words of the book of this
> prophecy, God shall take away his part out of the
> book of life, and out of the holy city, and from the
> things which are written in this book.
> —Revelation 22:18,19

We can count on God's Word because it is eternal. It has
no beginning of days and it has no ending of life. When the
earth was without form, and when darkness covered the
earth, the Word was.

We can count on God's Word because it does not change.
It is the same yesterday, today, and forever. Men change.
Doctrines change. Ideals change. But the Word of God never
changes!

In these perilous times, it is vital we know the purpose
of the Word is to destroy the works of the devil:

> He that committeth sin is of the devil; for the
> devil sinneth from the beginning. For this purpose
> the Son of God was manifested, that he might
> destroy the works of the devil.
> —1 John 3:8

Abraham trusted the Word of God and provided his

beloved son as a sacrifice. Today, God is saying to us, "Now it is your turn to make the sacrifice. Build yourself an altar. Climb up on that altar and lay down."

But you know what we do? We try to provide the sacrifice every other way but in the mountain of God. We do not ever go to the mountain of God. We cannot make the sacrifice unless we get in the mountain, because the sacrifice is provided in the mountain.

Years later, we find a man named David who had sinned. Because of his sin, a blight had come upon the entire nation of Israel. King David sat in sackcloth and ashes, and God said to him, "Go to Ornan's threshing floor."

The Bible says,

> Then the angel of the Lord commanded Gad to say to David, that David should go up, and set up an altar unto the Lord in the threshingfloor of Ornan the Jebusite.
>
> —1 Chronicles 21:18

Ornan's threshing floor was located on the same spot where Abraham had offered Isaac on Mount Moriah! We have to offer our sacrifices on the mountain of God.

But we have our own ideas about how to please God, don't we? For example, often we try to offer sacrifices with our good works. We go to church; we serve on the deacon board; we usher. We try to do all the good works. And God says, "Wait a minute. You are offering me a polluted sacrifice."

Our sacrifice does not become authentic until we say, "Take my hopes, my dreams, my plans, and I will still worship you, because you are my God. I know the truth of your Word, Lord, and I will not be moved from its truth."

We must refuse to cast away our confidence in God. We

must not take matters into our own hands, lest we produce Ishmaels. Remember, Ishmael was circumcised in the same way Isaac was. Ishmael had the sign of the covenant, yet he became a curse.

You can trust the Word of God. He will fulfill His Word to you. The only help God needs from us is to move "self" out of the way. The only way to do that is to lay our flesh on the altar and become a living sacrifice.

Throughout the ages, men have tried to wipe out every trace of the Bible—the written Word—from the face of the earth. They have ridiculed it, spit on it, banned it from their countries, burned it, tried to discredit it, and slandered it by calling it a book of myths and fairy tales. Even in some of our seminaries, professors deny that the Bible is the Word of God. Men have twisted it and perverted it with their doctrines. But in spite of all these attacks, the Word still stands! It has not lost its power.

From the very beginning, as the disciples began to speak forth the Word in the name of Jesus, Satan tried to stop them. The disciples were thrown in jail, beaten, and commanded not to speak or teach the Word. It did not stop God's Word.

Satan could not stop the Word from going forth. Instead, the Word of God increased. Paul, who was bound and thrown into prison for preaching the Word, wrote to Timothy:

> Remember that Jesus Christ of the seed of David was raised from the dead according to my gospel: Wherein I suffer trouble, as an evil doer, even unto bonds; but the word of God is not bound.
> —2 Timothy 2:8,9

God and His Word are inseparable! The Bible tells us perilous times will come and shake up the world in these last days. But God has not planned any defeats for us; He has us covered. As we fix our faith and trust in the Word of God, nothing can shake us.

God is preparing an end-time people who are so strong the devil will tremble in their presence, just as he trembled when Jesus addressed him.

No power of the enemy can defeat us as we fulfill the words of Jesus: "If ye abide in me, and my words abide in you, ye shall ask what ye will, and it shall be done unto you" (John 15:7).

Remember:

• The same power that spoke the sun, moon, and stars into existence;

• The same power that spoke forth the dry land, the forests, the mountains, and created the rivers and the oceans;

• The same power that spoke into creation all the animals, the birds, the fish, and all forms of life;

• The same power that spoke man into creation from the dust of the earth and breathed life into him;

• The same power of the Word is in us!

The Word which in the beginning was God; the Word which was and is God; the Word which created all things – became flesh.

Now that same living Word dwells within us. Praise be to the God of the Word!

There is many a life today which has no song. The most popular song for most of you would be:

'Where is that joy which once I knew, When first I loved the Lord?'

"Right behind you where you left it when you went to that card party; right where you left it when you began to go to the theater; right where you left it when you side-stepped and backslid; right where you left it when you began paying one hundred dollars for a dress and gave twenty-five cents to the Lord; right where you left it when you began to gossip.

—Billy Sunday, The Man and His Message

And she said, The Philistines be upon thee, Samson. And he awoke out of his sleep, and said, I will go out as at other times before, and shake myself. And he wist not that the Lord was departed from him.

—Judges 16:20

You have been going where you should not go, seeing what you should not see, and hearing what you should not hear.

—Pastor Rod Parsley

KEY 18:
AVOID THE LAP OF DELILAH

What happened to Samson to cause the Lord to depart from him? Samson went where he should not have gone: "Then went Samson to Gaza, and saw there an harlot, and went in unto her" (Judges 16:1).

When we go where we should not go, we are going to see what we should not see. When we go where we should not go, we are going to hear what we should not hear. When we go where we should not go, we are going to do what we should not do.

No one forced Samson to go; he went because he wanted to go. Do not ever let anyone, including the lying devil, dupe you with the pretense he made you or forced you into doing anything sinful.

The devil does not cause most of the trouble we go through. Most of the time, we cause our own problems.

As blood bought, Holy Ghost-filled, fire-baptized believers, we have no one to blame for our problems but ourselves. Samson had the same issues:

> And it was told the Gazites, saying, Samson is come hither. And they compassed him in, and laid wait for him all night in the gate of the city, and were quiet all the night, saying, In the morning, when it is

day, we shall kill him. And Samson lay till midnight, and arose at midnight, and took the doors of the gate of the city, and the two posts, and went away with them, bar and all, and put them upon his shoulders, and carried them up to the top of an hill that is before Hebron.

—Judges 16:2,3

In this passage, even though he was where he should not have been, Samson still had some power left! I imagine Samson repented all the way home, but the devil is relentless. He wants all the power we have.

Delilah, the devil's agent, wanted to take all Samson's power, so she asked him,

And Delilah said to Samson, Tell me, I pray thee, wherein thy great strength lieth, and wherewith thou mightest be bound to afflict thee.

—Judges 16:6

At first, Samson lied and told her to bind him with "seven green withs that were never dried" (v.7). When that failed, he told her to bind him with "new ropes that never were occupied" (v.11). But that failed. A third time she asked, and Samson told her to "weave the seven locks of my head with the web" (v.13).

That too failed, but Delilah was relentless. She "pressed him daily with her words, and urged him, so that his soul was vexed unto death" (v.16). As long as you live in the devil's territory—in the lap of Delilah—the devil will never give up on you until he has you.

Finally, Samson gave up and told Delilah what she wanted to know: "If I be shaven, then my strength will go from me, and I shall become weak, and be like any other man" (v.17). God made His power available to Samson, but he ultimately lost that power living in the lap of sin.

God has also given us His power. The Bible says, to as many as would receive Him, to them He gave power: "But as many as received him, to them gave he power to become the sons of God, even to them that believe on his name" (John 1:12).

Now, either He gave us power, or He is a liar. And if God is a liar, we should all throw our Bibles in a big bonfire. If we cannot have the power God said was available to us, then God is a liar.

Well, God is not a liar. The apostle Paul wrote,

> God forbid: yea, let God be true, but every man a liar; as it is written, That thou mightest be justified in thy sayings, and mightest overcome when thou art judged.
>
> —Romans 3:4

His power is available to as many as receive Jesus—and as many as stay out of the lap of sin.

He gave us the power to defeat the enemy! When? When we received Him. The apostle Peter told us,

> The Lord is not slack concerning his promise, as some men count slackness; but is longsuffering to us-ward, not willing that any should perish, but that all should come to repentance.
>
> —2 Peter 3:9

Only when Samson left the lap of Delilah and repented of his sin did God restore his strength:

> And Samson called unto the Lord, and said, O Lord God, remember me, I pray thee, and strength-

en me, I pray thee, only this once, O God, that I may be at once avenged of the Philistines for my two eyes.

—Judges 16:28

Today, if you are living in the lap of Delilah, get out while you still have the strength! Don't let the devil steal your power.

Commodore Vanderbilt had a fortune of over $200 million and one day when he was ill he sent for Dr. Deems. He asked him to sing for him that old song: 'Come, ye sinners, poor and needy, Come, ye wounded, sick and sore.'

The old Commodore tossed from side to side, looked around at the evidence of his wealth, and said: 'That is what I am, poor and needy.'

Who? Commodore Vanderbilt poor and needy with his $200 million? The foundation of that fabulous fortune was laid by him when he poled a yawl from New York to Staten Island and picked up pennies for doing it.

The foundation of the immense Astor fortune was laid by John Jacob Astor when he went out and bought fur and hides from trappers and put the money in New York real estate.

The next day on the street, one man said to another: 'Have you heard the news? Commodore Vanderbilt is dead.' 'How much did he leave?,' 'He left nothing at all.'

Naked you came into this world, and naked you will crawl out of it. You brought nothing into the world, and you will take nothing out. And if you have put the pack screws on the poor and piled up a pile of gold as big as a house, you cannot take it with you. It wouldn't do you any good if you could, because it would melt.

—Billy Sunday, The Man and His Message

Nay, in all these things we are more than conquerors through him that loved us.

—Romans 8:37

KEY 19:
DON'T QUIT

Stay faithful to God. Never quit—never allow bitterness or anger to set in your spirit—and your life will become a living temple to glorify His holy name.

—Pastor Rod Parsley

From the time he was seventeen-years-old God gave Joseph, the son of Jacob, the ability to interpret the meaning of dreams. Joseph was a faithful and godly man who was loved dearly by his father—so much so his own brothers despised and hated him:

And when his brethren saw that their father loved him more than all his brethren, they hated him, and could not speak peaceably unto him.

—Genesis 37:4

So deep was the jealousy of Joseph's brothers they "conspired against him to slay him" (Genesis 37:18). Finally, instead of killing him, they decided to cast young Joseph into a deep pit.

Joseph was soon taken out of the pit and sold into slavery to Midianite merchants for twenty pieces of silver. The merchants then brought Joseph into Egypt, where they sold him to Potiphar, an officer of Pharaoh and the captain of the guard.

Throughout all these undeserved events, there is nothing written anywhere in the Bible to indicate Joseph complained at all. As far as we know, he never even asked, "God, I have served you faithfully. I love you. So why are you doing these things to me?"

Joseph never quit in His service and love of the Lord. Joseph never uttered one negative word against God. He trusted God and remained faithful despite the perilous times in his own life.

When Joseph was brought into Egypt, so strong was his relationship with God the circumstances the devil intended for evil were turned around for good. Before long "the Lord was with Joseph, and he was a prosperous man; and he was in the house of his master the Egyptian" (Genesis 39:2).

So faithful was Joseph to God even his heathen master took note of his love of the Lord:

> And his master saw that the Lord was with him, and that the Lord made all that he did to prosper in his hand. And Joseph found grace in his sight, and he served him: and he made him overseer over his house, and all that he had he put into his hand.
> —Genesis 39:3,4

The enemy was not going to stand to see Joseph prosper, so the devil used Potiphar's wife as an instrument to destroy Joseph:

> And he (Potiphar) left all that he had in Joseph's hand; and he knew not ought he had, save the bread

which he did eat. And Joseph was a goodly person, and well favoured. And it came to pass after these things, that his master's wife cast her eyes upon Joseph; and she said, Lie with me. But he refused, and said unto his master's wife, Behold, my master wotteth not what is with me in the house, and he hath committed all that he hath to my hand.

—Genesis 39:6-8

Joseph refused the woman's advances. But Potiphar's wife would not be deterred. Like the devil, she was persistent to achieve her wicked end.

Again Joseph refused, this time fleeing while she tugged at his garment, ripping it off of him. Potiphar's wife was so angry at Joseph's rejection she lied to her husband, claiming Joseph had entered her room and tried to sleep with her, leaving his garment behind as he fled from the bedroom while she cried out in protest.

As a result of his wife's false accusations, Potiphar tossed Joseph into prison. But Joseph still did not quit on God! He continued to be a godly man—even though his brothers had rejected him, even though he had been thrown into a pit, even though he had been sold into slavery, and now, even though he was thrown into prison for something he did not do!

Joseph kept his eyes focused on God: "But the Lord was with Joseph, and shewed him mercy, and gave him favour in the sight of the keeper of the prison" (Genesis 39:21).

Do you see the pattern here? God was taking things meant for evil and was converting them into events to be used for good. Why? Because Joseph remained faithful. Despite perilous circumstances, he never once quit on God!

His brothers sold Joseph into slavery—yet Joseph became the head of a rich household in Egypt. Potiphar's wife lied about Joseph and sent him to prison—yet in prison, he prospered "because the Lord was with him, and that which he did, the Lord made it to prosper" (Genesis 39:23).

While in prison, Joseph interpreted dreams for Potiphar's butler and baker, and both dreams came to pass. Despite the chief butler's promise to remember Joseph, he forgot him. Once again, Joseph could have become bitter at the chief butler's broken promise, and quit on God. For two more years, Joseph remained in jail.

He could have become bitter then. He could have been angry with God. But Joseph remained faithful, refusing to quit on God, no matter how bad his current circumstances seemed.

Two years later, when Pharaoh sent for Joseph to interpret his dreams, Joseph humbly stated, "It is not in me: God shall give Pharaoh an answer of peace" (Genesis 41:16).

After two years, Joseph was still serving God—he did not quit!

God gave Joseph the ability to interpret the dreams, and he warned that Egypt would have seven good years for harvest, followed by seven years of famine. Joseph devised a plan to store wheat during times of plenty so Egypt would be prepared for the time of famine. Pharaoh appointed Joseph in charge of the project, saying "only in the throne will I be greater than thou" (Genesis 41:40).

Because Joseph did not quit on God during his times of peril, God continually gave him favor, and eventually blessed the latter end of his life even more than the former.

You know the rest of the story. Joseph eventually sold wheat to his brothers—the very men who sold him into slavery! Joseph's brothers were sure he would kill them when their father Jacob died, but Joseph reassured them,

And Joseph said unto them, Fear not: for am I in the place of God? But as for you, ye thought evil against me; but God meant it unto good, to bring to pass, as it is this day, to save much people alive. Now therefore fear ye not: I will nourish you, and your little ones. And he comforted them, and spake kindly unto them.

—Genesis 50:19-21

These are the actions of a man unmoved by his circumstances—a man who never gave up on God during the toughest of times.

Joseph died at age 110, a godly man who refused to quit through the most perilous and frustrating of times. When he was sold into slavery—he did not quit. When he was falsely accused and imprisoned—he did not quit. When he was forgotten—he did not quit.

The devil's strategy for your life is to make you quit. He will bring trouble into your life, hoping in your desperation you will accuse God as the source of your trouble and quit. The devil hopes to wear you down through frustration, anger, and desperation, until finally you give up on God. But God never gives up on you. He has you covered, and He is committed to protecting His children.

You and I must follow Joseph's example. We must stay faithful to God when trouble comes. We must trust God despite our circumstances. He will always lead us out of our trials.

Stay faithful to God. Never quit. Never allow bitterness or anger to settle in your spirit and rob you of the blessings God intends for you.

Like Joseph, in every situation—good or bad—let your life become a living temple to glorify His holy name.

You do not have the Spirit of a quitter living inside you; you have the Spirit of the only man in history to conquer death. You have the Spirit of a winner – the Spirit of Jesus Christ inside you.

—Pastor Rod Parsley

Jesus walked, blood-soaked, beaten, and battered on that rough and rocky road to Calvary—kicked and prodded through the dirty streets of Jerusalem. If He were ever going to quit, that would have been the time for Him to do it.

But when Judas betrayed him with a kiss, Jesus did not turn from God.

When Peter denied Him three times, He did not turn from God.

When Pilate washed his hands of this innocent man, He did not turn from God.

When the skin on his back was viciously ripped away by a whip tipped with bits of bone and shards of glass, when a mock crown of sharp thorns punctured his brow, He did not turn from God.

When huge spikes were driven into His hands and feet, He did not turn from God.

Three days after His death, Jesus broke the bondage of the grave and rose from the dead, declaring loudly to the world, "I am the Christ, the Son of the Living God, and not even death can turn me from God."

Today, that same victorious Christ who overcomes all circumstances lives inside you. You have the Spirit of a winner—the Spirit of Jesus Christ living inside you. And you don't have to quit.

As you read this book, you may feel like giving up. You may feel like the crushing circumstances of your deteriorating marriage are too much to bear. You may feel like your monthly bills have become so huge and so hopeless there is no way out. You may be convinced your unsaved child is so firmly rooted in addiction nothing will ever make a difference. You may be unemployed with no prospects for a job, and mourn the financial security you thought you had.

I have news for you. You are a child of God, and God does not quit!

Take your eyes off your circumstances. Like Joseph, do not look at the confines of your prison walls; see the magnitude of your God. Do not look at the depth of the pit you are in; recognize the power of God to lead you out!

Do not look at the false accusations of others and say, "Woe is me." Instead, praise God for His protection as He brings you through the fire.

You are not going to quit because greater is He that is in you that he that is in the world.

When you give your life to Him, when you die to yourself, He resurrects you into His glory.

God will never quit on you.

Be out and out for God. Have a heart-to-heart talk with some people and win them to Christ. The first recorded words of Jesus are these: 'Wist ye not that I must be about my Father's business?'

—Luke 2:49b

The trouble is we are too lackadaisical in religion, indifferent, dead, and lifeless. That is the spirit of the committees today in the church. I think the multitude in the church will have to get converted themselves before they can lead anyone else to Christ. It is my firm conviction, after many years of experience in the work, that half the people in the church have never been converted, have never been born again.

I take up a bottle of water, uncork it and take a drink. That is experimental. One sip of water can convince me more of water's power to satisfy thirst than 40,000 books written on the subject.

You know quinine water is bitter because you have experimented; you know fire will burn because you have experimented; you know ice will freeze your hands because you have experimented.

A man must experience religion to know God.

—Billy Sunday, The Man and His Message

The youngest babe in Christ is much more than a match for the devil.

—Pastor Rod Parsley

Key 20:
Reflect the Christ Life

One thing is certain: light will always dispel darkness. No night was ever so deep dawn could not dispel it. The apostle John wrote, "For whatsoever is born of God overcometh the world: and this is the victory that overcometh the world, even our faith" (1 John 5:4).

You do not overcome darkness because of what you have done; you overcome darkness because of who you are in Christ.

I have two children at home. As long as I can breathe and move, they will always overcome hunger. They are born of the Parsley family, and they will overcome whatever Rod Parsley can overcome.

I will nurture and protect my wife and children because of who they are—members of my family. As long as I can stand, no one is ever going to hurt them, and they are never going to go hungry!

You are a member of God's family. God lovingly stands over you, around you, and lives personally within you. As long as you belong to God's family, no enemy is ever going to hurt you, and you are never going to go hungry or unprotected.

Jesus said,

> The thief cometh not, but for to steal, and to kill,

and to destroy: I am come that they might have life,
and that they might have it more abundantly.

—John 10:10

You are in the family of Christ, and God wants to take
care of you and give you abundant life.

Now, let me be very frank here. I have heard many
preachers use John 10:10 to claim God wants us to totally
prosper in all areas, all the time! But that is not the case if
you view prosperity and abundance through the world's
eyes.

Joseph enjoyed God's abundance while he was in prison
because he knew whom he served, and served Him with a
glad heart.

Abundant life in God's eyes does not mean everything
that discomforts your flesh is of the devil, and everything
that comforts your flesh is of God. It means we participate in
the nature and the life of Christ, and we are abundant in all
circumstances—even though they may be perilous!

Joseph enjoyed God's abundance because he knew the
nature of God, and rejoiced in the privilege of being able to
serve Him.

In the family of God, we rejoice with Jesus Christ as we
share in His suffering, and we rejoice when we share His resurrection from the dead.

The true representation of your character is not how you
respond on the mountaintop. The measure of your character
is how you respond when you face circumstances like Joseph
faced—how you respond to the raging fires and floods of
life.

Television has become the medium that dictates its false,
perverted values and morals to America. But television does
not reflect Christ. To be more like Christ, you must go to
another source—the Word of God! Let the Word be the mir-

174

ror of what the Christ life is to you.

You say, "I want to live a full life." And Jesus replies, "If you want to live, know that this is not a fantasy world. If you want to live, then you first must die. Die to yourself. Die to your will. Die to your way, and let my Christlikeness be produced in you."

That is the only way.

> Do not see how close you can come to the world and still be in Christ. Rather, see how close you can get to God and still be in this world.
>
> —Pastor Rod Parsley

Scripture consistently warns us to be careful to avoid evil and the places where evil abounds.

Along the bank of the river of God's will is the place where water and land meet. You would be better to stay on dry terra firma than to stir around in the mud of the shallows.

God despises those who are lukewarm. Jesus's message to the church in Laodicea was,

> I know thy works, that thou art neither cold nor hot: I would thou wert cold or hot. So then because thou art lukewarm, and neither cold nor hot, I will spue thee out of my mouth.
>
> —Revelation 3:15,16

I heard a story about a little girl who fell out of bed during the night. His father ran to comfort her, and then asked her why she fell. The girl responded, "I guess I stayed too close to where I got in."

You and I often stay too close to where we got into this Christian life, don't we? We court temptation despite biblical commands to flee it. Do not try to see how close you can come to the world and still be in Christ. Rather, see how close you can draw to God and still function in this world. Satan's works will be destroyed as you manifest Jesus in your life. Manifest Christlikeness in both the good times and the bad, with those who are loveable and those who are unlovable.

You and I need to be like Jesus in every area of our lives. When Jesus was persecuted, He asked His Heavenly Father to forgive His accusers, and to release of any guilt those who drove the nails into His hands. Let Christ's life come out in you—that is what destroys the works of the enemy.

The apostle John wrote,

> He that committeth sin is of the devil; for the devil sinneth from the beginning. For this purpose the Son of God was manifested, that he might destroy the works of the devil.
>
> —1 John 3:8

Christ in you will annihilate the works of the devil.

King David prayed,

> Keep back thy servant also from presumptuous sins; let them not have dominion over me: then shall I be upright, and I shall be innocent from the great transgression.
>
> —Psalm 19:13

In other words, David was saying, "Lord, deliver me from the idolatrous sin of presumption that I would think You are something You are not."

Manifesting Christlikeness means manifesting who Christ is—in you. It means manifesting humility. It means forgiving the unforgivable, and loving those who do not deserve your love. It means being willing to give up something temporal to gain something eternal.

Because of your Christlikeness, because you are born of God, you can overcome anything God can. As the apostle Paul wrote, "Nay, in all these things we are more than conquerors through him that loved us" (Romans 8:37).

CONCLUSION:
TROUBLED TIMES, SUPERNATURAL STRENGTH

You and I are in the final moments of spiritual history. This is the perilous, troubled time foretold in Scripture: "This know also, that in the last days perilous times shall come" (2 Timothy 3:1).

But while the world is crumbling in moral and financial chaos, you do not need to be troubled. By implementing these twenty keys for God's protection, you now have hope beyond the troubled times of humanity! Truly, He has you covered!

As a spirit man, you are not dictated to and dominated by human limitations. You can rise above the seen into the unseen.

Armed with these strategies, you can face all temptation, conquer cancer, cast off enemy attack and overcome any financial obstacle, in His supernatural strength!

The world is not going to get better; it is going to get worse. But as you put these twenty keys to work, you will have the supernatural strength and power of God protecting and covering you in the midst of troubled times.

He will meet your every need! You may be facing the greatest trials and conflicts of your life—but you are not facing them alone!

Yes, God is shaking this world, but through making

these keys for protection a part of your life, you will emerge victorious!

Do not let your natural circumstances dictate your spiritual altitude. Remember, Jesus went into the grave and came out victorious on the other side. He set the pattern. You are His child, and He has given you the same supernatural strength to overcome every circumstance in your life.

You have been born into a supernatural kingdom that cannot be moved. It is only when you step outside the kingdom of God that you have anything to fear in this world. God will preserve you in the midst of trouble.

In the last days, God promises to pour out His Spirit on all flesh:

> And it shall come to pass in the last days, saith God, I will pour out of my Spirit upon all flesh: and your sons and your daughters shall prophesy, and your young men shall see visions, and your old men shall dream dreams: And on my servants and on my handmaidens I will pour out in those days of my Spirit; and they shall prophesy: And I will shew wonders in heaven above, and signs in the earth beneath; blood, and fire, and vapour of smoke.
> —Acts 2:17-19

God is turning up the heat, but you will be swimming in the cool pool of the living water of the Holy Spirit!

Remember, it does not matter what circumstances you are facing today, or what circumstances you will encounter tomorrow. If you will apply God's keys for protection to your life, you will have the supernatural strength to be victorious in every circumstance!

Times have always been perilous, but this is "the perilous time!" The Sept. 11, 2001, terrorist attacks on America are a graphic reminder that we are living in the end times. Today we are living with the knowledge that the remnants of the group responsible for those hideous acts are actively laying in wait for the opportunity to duplicate them. A war is raging in the spirit between good and evil, heaven and hell. But God has not left us defenseless. He has given His people a series of divinely sculpted tactics in His Word to defeat the devil's demonic devices.

Church, we are God's children, and He will protect us. He has us covered!

NOTES:

About the Author

ROD PARSLEY, bestselling author of more than 60 books, is the dynamic Pastor of World Harvest Church in Columbus, Ohio, a church with worldwide ministries and a global outreach. As a highly sought-after crusade and conference speaker whom God has raised up as a prophetic voice to America and the world, Parsley is calling people to Jesus Christ through the good news of the Gospel.

He oversees Bridge of Hope Missions, World Harvest Preparatory School, World Harvest Bible College and the television broadcast Breakthrough, a Christian television and radio show seen by millions and broadcast to nearly 200 countries around the world, including a potential viewing audience of 97% of the homes in the United States and 78% in Canada. Breakthrough is carried on 1,400 stations and cable affiliates, including the Trinity Broadcasting Network, the Canadian Vision Network, Armed Forces Radio and Television Network and in several countries spanning the globe.

Parsley's refreshingly direct style encourages Christians to examine and eradicate sin from their lives. A fearless champion of living God's way, Parsley follows the high standard set by Jesus Christ and compels his readers to do the sameParsley has authored several books including the number one bestseller On the Brink, bestsellers The Day Before Eternity, No Dry Season, No More Crumbs and the popular devotional Daily Breakthrough. He and his wife Joni have two children, Ashton and Austin.

OTHER BOOKS BY ROD PARSLEY

At The Cross, Where Healing Begins
Ancient Wells, Living Water
Could It Be?
Daily Breakthrough
The Day Before Eternity
He Came First
No Dry Season (Bestseller)
No More Crumbs (Bestseller)
On the Brink (#1 Bestseller)
Repairers of the Breach

For more information about Breakthrough,
World Harvest Church,
World Harvest Bible College,
Harvest Preparatory School,
or to receive a product list of the many books,
CD's and DVD's by
Rod Parsley, write or call:

Breakthrough/World Harvest Church
P.O. Box 32932
Columbus, OH 43232-0932
(614) 837-1990 (Office)

World Harvest Bible College
P.O. Box 32901
Columbus, OH 43232-0901
(614) 837-4088
www.worldharvestbiblecollege.org

Harvest Preparatory School
P.O. Box 32903
Columbus, OH 43232-0903
(614) 837-1990
www.harvestprep.org

If you need prayer, Breakthrough Prayer Warriors
are ready to pray with you
24 hours a day, 7 days a week at:
(614) 837-3232